Writing & Selling the
YA Novel

K.L. GOING

Author of *Saint Iggy* and *Fat Kid Rules the World*,
a Michael L. Printz Honor Book

WRITER'S DIGEST BOOKS
Cincinnati, Ohio
www.writersdigest.com

12 11 10 09 08   5 4 3 2 1

Distributed in Canada by Fraser Direct, 100 Armstrong Avenue, Georgetown, Ontario, Canada L7G 5S4; Distributed in the U.K. and Europe by David & Charles, Brunel House, Newton Abbot, Devon, TQ12 4PU, England, E-mail: postmaster@davidandcharles.co.uk; Distributed in Australia by Capricorn Link, P.O. Box 704, Windsor, NSW 2756 Australia.

Library of Congress Cataloging-in-Publication Data
Going, K. L. (Kelly L.)
 Writing and selling the YA novel / by K.L. Going.
   p. cm.
 ISBN-13: 978-1-58297-515-3 (pbk. : alk. paper)
 ISBN-10: 1-58297-515-9 (pbk. : alk. paper)
 1. Young adult fiction--Authorship. I. Title.
 PN3377.G55 2008
 808.06'8--dc22   2007049187

Edited by Alice Pope

Cover Designed by Eric West

Designed by Terri Woesner

production coordinated
by Mark Griffin

Cover illustration ©
Rob Melnychuk/Getty Images

fw
F+W PUBLICATIONS, INC.

Dedication

For Kathy, who has shared her wisdom with generosity, patience, laughter, and kindness.

Acknowledgments

There are so many people who helped make this book possible. First and foremost I'd like to thank my editor, Alice Pope, who made this a fun book to work on from start to finish. I'd also like to thank my agent, Ginger Knowlton, for being open to every possibility, and everyone at Curtis Brown, Ltd. from whom I learned so much. Thanks to Dustin Adams for his knowledgeable critique and Carol Daley for her expertise. Thanks to YALSA for the work that they do and for answering my questions. My deepest gratitude goes out to all the teens who filled out my Teen Panel Questionnaire, to all the librarians and teachers who helped with distribution, and to the YA authors who blogged to spread the word. Your contribution added so much. And of course, when you're writing a book about writing and selling the YA novel, you're immediately in debt to all the authors who have produced the wonderful works of fiction that populate this genre and are mentioned in the pages of this book. Thanks for all the stories I loved as a teen and continue to love as an adult.

About the Author

K.L. Going is the award-winning author of books for children and teens. Her first novel, *Fat Kid Rules the World*, was named a Michael Printz honor book by the American Library Association, as well as one of the Best Books for Young Adults from the past decade. Her books have been Junior Library Guild selections, Booksense picks, *Publishers Weekly*, and School Library Journal Best Books, and state award winners. They've been published in many countries around the world.

Going has worked as an assistant to literary agents at Curtis Brown, Ltd. in New York; a manager of an independent bookstore; a reading teacher; and a freelance book doctor, so she offers a unique perspective to aspiring writers, exploring the world of YA fiction from every angle. You can visit her at www.klgoing.com.

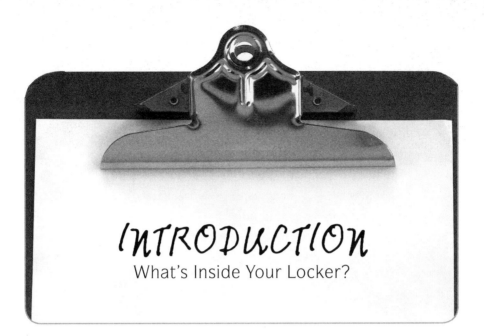

INTRODUCTION

What's Inside Your Locker?

Remember the first day of school?

Can you recall the feeling of walking into each new classroom wondering which of your friends would be there, where you would sit, and what the teacher would be like? Well, this is a school for two—you and me. You can sit wherever you'd like, but I have to warn you: Although you'll change subjects from period to period, I'll be your teacher for every single class. That's why I thought I'd start by telling you a little bit about me and my teaching style.

First of all, I hope you'll be comfortable, but do have your pen and paper ready because we will be using it. I believe the only way to learn how to write is by practicing again and again and again. So, yes, there will be lots of homework.

Some of you might be thinking, "Uh-oh, this teacher is strict. Homework on the first day of class?" But you can relax. There won't be any homework until the school day officially starts, and although I am strict (you'll read more about discipline later), I'm also one of those teachers who really cares about her subject.

And her students.

So here's a little bit of information about me.

I like to tell people that I know books from every angle. It's true.

The daughter of a librarian, I grew up reading aloud with my parents from the time I was very small. I started out sitting on their laps, listening to the sounds of the words. As I grew older, my whole family passed the books from person to person, each one taking his or her turn to read a passage.

It was this love of reading that prompted me to accept a volunteer position after college working with adult students on basic reading skills. Reading had always been something I adored, so why not share that with others?

I worked as an adult literacy tutor for two and a half years before returning to my home in New York. The question "What should I do next?" was never far from my mind, but fortunately for me, a friend recommended I apply for a job at a literary agency. To my surprise, I got the position. This was the start of almost five years at Curtis Brown, Ltd., where I was privileged to work with many top literary agents. I watched manuscripts move from unpolished gems to the bookshelves of Barnes & Noble, from the slush pile to a contract, and from an agent's desk back to the author for another try.

This was invaluable experience, especially since I was also writing my own books. I wrote my first full-length novel in high school, but I was always writing "just for fun," lacking the confidence to submit my work. Even while working in publishing, it was still a long time before I showed my writing to anyone. I was convinced that as soon as people saw what a horrible writer I was they'd lose confidence in my ability to critique manuscripts or judge query letters and my job would be at stake.

Sharing my work was a risk, just as it is for you, but I'm certainly glad I did it. My first published novel, *Fat Kid Rules the World*, was named a Michael L. Printz honor book and has been a Junior Library Guild selection and a YALSA Best Book for Young Adults. I now have four novels published with more under contract, and my books have been translated into Japanese, Korean, and Italian. Each book has been made into an audiobook, and I've even had a movie option for *Fat Kid Rules the World*!

Of course, getting published doesn't mean you necessarily get rich (more on that in math class), so what have I been doing besides writing books?

Well, I couldn't work full time and still produce novels on deadline, so I left my job at the literary agency and got a job at, you guessed it, a local bookstore. Where else? For the next two years I stood behind the counter watching customers browse the shelves, hand selling my favorite titles, sadly boxing up books for returns then happily ordering new ones from publishers' catalogs, and occasionally catching the unsuspecting customer checking out my own titles when they were on display.

I've followed my books from start to finish, moving from reading to teaching to agenting to selling, and all along I've continued to pursue my greatest passion—writing. Now I write, speak at conferences, visit schools and libraries, and critique manuscripts.

Do I know books from every angle? Well, I'm certain there are one or two I haven't covered—so to help me out, I have some wonderful teaching assistants ready to take up the slack. At the end of every chapter you'll hear directly from teens all across the country about every subject we discuss. If there's one thing you'll hear from me again and again in this book, it's that teens are smart, articulate, and know their minds. So how could I not let them speak for themselves?

Participating teens come from a school in New Mexico, a soccer team in New Hampshire, libraries all across America, teen reading Web sites, and numerous individuals who responded to my request for teens ages twelve through eighteen willing to fill out a questionnaire about teen reading. Responses were wonderful, and it was difficult to choose which answers to quote, but I've tried to choose the responses that best represent the majority, while at the same time giving you an idea of how diverse teens are in their opinions. I can't wait to share the wit and wisdom of today's teenagers with you.

So, what kind of teacher will I be?

Hopefully the kind who can share real-world knowledge and inspire you to go farther than you thought possible. I've been privileged to see publishing from the inside out, and I'm excited to share my experiences with you. Now, if you're ready to start your school day and learn more about writing novels for young adults, let's open up your locker and see what's inside.

Writing books for publication is not an easy task. There are many authors competing for a limited number of slots on each publisher's list. How can you make sure your book catches an editor's attention? How can you be certain the material you've produced is well written? Is there a magic formula for success?

We all wish such a formula existed, but writing is a personal journey that takes a lot of hard work and dedication. The material you create will naturally reflect your own style, voice, and life experiences, and there's no way to guarantee that what you have to offer is what a publisher will be looking for at the time you submit your work. That's a truth that cannot be sugarcoated.

However, having said that, I can assure you that the more you learn, the more you increase your odds of success. There are many tools you can use to improve your skills, make your work more marketable, and best of all, help you create stories that readers will return to again and again.

Here are a few of them:

- determination
- perseverance
- creativity
- intelligence
- willingness to explore
- ability to practice
- learning from the experience of others
- Web sites
- magazines
- conferences
- writers' groups
- reading

These are just a few of the tools within your grasp. Undoubtedly, everyone's locker is different, and you surely have some opportunities that are uniquely yours. Intimate knowledge of your subject matter? A friend in the publishing business? Experience writing in other fields? Take time to look around and inventory what you have at your disposal. Don't discount anything that might help you along your path. That teenager lurking around your living room just might be the perfect source of inspiration.

Oh, and here's one more very important tool:

Your schedule.

Books like this can be invaluable because they not only allow you to carve out time in your busy life to study your craft, they also offer a comprehensive overview of everything you need to know to succeed.

So, here's what your school day will look like:

Homeroom: Here, we'll discuss your motivation for writing teen books. This is the time to look at how YA books differ from their adult or juvenile counterparts, and see what defines YA literature. Plus, I'll reveal my number one, most important piece of advice.

1ˢᵗ Period: History. Names and dates won't be dull when it comes to learning the history of books written for teenagers. Knowing where YA literature started and what has been accomplished by the authors who came before you can enrich your stories and allow you to innovate.

2ⁿᵈ Period: Gym. Many of us loved or hated gym class with a passion when we were in school, and isn't strong emotion exactly what fuels a good book? Here we'll explore what makes an idea great, where ideas come from, and how to implement them once you've found an idea you want to work with.

3ʳᵈ Period: English. I don't know about you, but English was always my favorite class. If there's one thing I love it's a good book, and good books are full of great characters. A memorable character will linger in a reader's mind long after she's finished reading. Learning to create and develop interesting personalities is essential to storytelling, and there's no better place to practice your skills than English class.

4ᵗʰ Period: Lunch. Isn't there more to a good story than characters? The characters have to *do* something, don't they? That's where lunch comes in. In the lunchroom alliances are formed, gossip is rampant, and cliques are everywhere. Someone is almost always in tears or in the process of breaking up with a boyfriend or girlfriend. In short, lunch means action, and action means plot.

5ᵗʰ Period: Social Studies. After lunch you'll proceed to social studies, where we'll take an in-depth look at setting. We'll discuss what role location plays in stories and how it can be used to affect plot and characters. Do you know which details can bring a location to life? If not, have your notebook ready.

6ᵗʰ Period: Study Hall. Narrative voice and point of view are two qualities of YA literature that have stood out over the years. In study hall you'll learn how you can make your teen voices sound realistic and how to figure out the best way to tell a given story. Learning about narration techniques will help you make good decisions. What does this require? Time! Good thing you've got study hall.

7ᵗʰ Period: Science. According to the *Oxford English Dictionary*, science is a branch of knowledge requiring systematic study and an expert's skillful technique. Skillful technique is what editing is all about. Very few of us (if any!) produce polished material in our first drafts. Learning how to improve what you write can make the difference between a manuscript that makes it to an editor's desk and one that gets lost in the slush pile.

8ᵗʰ Period: Math. How many of you dreaded math class when you were in school? But as a writer, you'll love it, because this is where we talk about money! Yes, writers can and do make money. Here's where you'll perfect your query letter, decide whether you're looking for an agent or an editor, and research the best marketplace for your material. You'll also learn the basics of negotiating a solid contract.

9th Period: Shop Class. In your school, was shop class reserved for the kids who smoked in the bathrooms and wore black leather jackets all year round? Or maybe shop class meant computers and learning the most up-to-date technology. Maybe you were one of those kids who waited all day for a chance to get your hands dirty, or the artist who made statements in the only class that allowed you to create. Regardless, there's no better place to talk shop than shop class. Here's where we'll discuss swearing, drugs, sex, slang, technology, and all the other ever-changing hot-button issues unique to the teen market. We'll also look at marketing your book once it gets published.

Sound like a lot to learn? Relax. You've got all the tools you require in your writing locker. You can progress at your own pace, taking all the time you need before moving on to the next class. In fact, I encourage you to do each of the homework assignments you receive, not because they'll be graded, but because practicing your skills is the best way to improve them.

So, if you're ready to go, the morning bell is ringing …

HOMEROOM
Time to Get Motivated

What's your most vivid memory from high school? How about middle school? Can you recall where you sat in ninth-grade social studies? Does the smell of the biology room still linger somewhere in your subconscious? What was your favorite class? Who was your best friend? Your worst enemy? Were you homeschooled? What's the one thing you know now that you wish you'd known back then?

If you've made it to homeroom today it's because you want to write novels for young adults. Congratulations! This is a wonderful goal, worthy of many hours in the classroom. Writing for young adults is an expanding field attracting some top authors. If you're looking to break into this market, you're off to a great start. Studying the craft is essential for success, and knowing who you are as a writer and who your audience is can help you begin your career with a solid foundation.

But maybe you're not so sure you've come to the right place.

 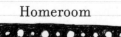

Maybe you've tiptoed into homeroom because someone put it on your schedule, but you're not certain where you should sit or whether you really belong here at all. Perhaps you think you're too old to go back to school. Maybe you can't answer any of the questions at the beginning of this chapter. The smell of the biology room? That was years ago! Is remembering your locker combination a prerequisite for success?

Why would someone choose to write for the teen market anyway?

If you want to write a young adult (YA) novel this is the number one question to address. Writing takes a lot of stamina. It requires hours of solitary work, creating and recreating characters, plot, and setting. It takes energy and enthusiasm, and trust me, if you aren't entirely in love with your book and its characters, you'll never make it through round after round of editing. So it's important to be sure that the work you create is coming from your heart.

Does this mean you can't experiment? Try out different voices and styles? Absolutely not! Experimentation is essential if you're going to learn what works for you, but you can save yourself a lot of time by understanding the field you're delving into. Learning about other books similar to the one you're writing can spark ideas, shape the choices you make, and maybe even influence the way you approach your novel.

In homeroom we'll explore the defining characteristics of the YA novel, the reasons someone might (or might not!) want to write for teens, and what you'll need to know to get started.

WHY WRITE FOR TEENS?

Okay, class, settle down. Let's go around the room and share why we're all here today.

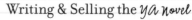

Remember when you were a kid and adults asked this question? Back then the answer was almost always, "Because I have to be." Only that was never what you said out loud. Instead, it was necessary to come up with platitudes to please the teacher.

I chose this class because I really want to learn about economics.
I'm here so I can become a well-rounded individual.
I truly love science.

Sometimes those platitudes were true, but more often they were just what you said in order to get through the activity you'd been forced to attend. Now that we're adults, we get to enjoy the freedom of choosing our activities and arranging our schedules exactly as we'd like. We have unlimited choices and can usually do exactly what we want.

Or can we?

When was the last time you stifled a yawn at a meeting? Have you ever wished you could throw your daily planner out the window? Are you constantly promising yourself you'll slow down only to find it never seems to happen?

The truth is, no matter how old we get, we share much in common with teenagers. The experiences and emotions of those years never disappear completely, and that's part of the reason I love writing for teens. No matter how old you are, you still experience emotions that are the same as when you were younger, but now you possess more life experience than you did when you were a kid, so you can put them in a different context. Writing books for young adults is a unique opportunity to channel both familiar emotions and unfamiliar experiences, exploring ideas and issues that are meaningful to teens yet still relevant in your own life.

Of course, this can be a challenge because, while the core emotional truths stay the same, there are also a lot of things that have changed since you were in school, even if you graduated only a few years ago. Think of all the things that are different now than they were when you were in high school or middle school:

- your body
- technology
- language
- relationships to friends and family
- how you spend your time
- your goals
- the world around you

This list could go on and on, and maybe that seems intimidating, but it can also be exciting. Writing books for young adults allows us to revisit the world in a new way.

If you're feeling out of touch, don't panic. Television, movies, music, and people-watching are easy ways to observe what's going on in the world of teens. If you don't know any teenagers personally, go see the top-rated teen movies, or read *Teen Vogue* or *Seventeen*. Better yet, stop by some forums online, or get a MySpace or Facebook page. Just beware of judging adolescents by their covers. You certainly wouldn't want teens to base their assumptions about adults on the hit Monday night TV show or the latest romantic comedy. And beware of writing your book with the sole intent to reach a "hip" portion of the demographic. Books are first and foremost art and entertainment, and books for teens are no exceptions. The best YA books can appeal to almost any age group and almost any type of teen because they use strong writing to tell meaningful stories with well-developed characters.

Many people underestimate teenagers, but I think the average teen is far more complex than we think. Most teens are already reading adult books, so the intent of the teen novel isn't to "write down" to them, but rather to give them a body of literature that is uniquely their own. Our teenage years can be tumultuous ones. Teenagers are on the brink of adulthood, and their understanding of the world can be simultaneously very broad and very limited. Some teens live sheltered lives, yet others catapult forward, dealing with experiences and issues most adults would be hard-pressed to navigate. Books for teenagers must tap into both ends of this spectrum.

Think about this: Have you ever watched a performer standing on stage belting out songs to a huge audience and thought that you wouldn't have the courage and composure to do the same? Have you then found out the performer was just fifteen or sixteen years old? Teens are capable of amazing accomplishments, yet they are also just beginning to experiment with adult roles. They're constantly shaping their identities and redefining how they interact with the ever-changing world around them.

This is the deep well from which YA literature draws. Our audience is astute, demanding, inquisitive, and always in flux. Their openness to diversity of form and content allows the YA writer a nearly limitless canvas. As author Bruce Brooks says in Marc Aronson's *Exploding the Myths: The Truth About Teens and Reading*, "Someone who does not share the fundamental conviction that these [teens] are people of profound integrity, intelligence, and feeling ought to be a writer, editor, publisher, critic, librarian, or bookseller for someone else. Young adults deserve our best regard and our best literature."

I believe they are getting it.

Young adult writers today are constantly exploring the teenage world, giving it the layers and complexity it deserves. Understanding what other authors have created and analyzing how they've accomplished it can be an important learning experience and may even remind you of a few things from your own past that you think you've forgotten. It will certainly help you determine whether this is the market you are best suited to write for.

Writing for teens isn't easy. It's a balancing act—weighing what's relevant with what's timeless—but if you can do this, you can succeed in any genre.

DEFINING YOUNG ADULT

Maybe you're thinking all this sounds great but wondering how you'll know when the book you're reading or working on is a YA novel. Maybe what you're writing is really a middle-grade novel, or perhaps it's more suited to adults. Sure, teen novels are exciting and challenging, but what exactly *are* they?

This question isn't as easy to answer as you might think.

With almost every genre of literature you can create a list of definable characteristics, and while there will always be exceptions, the exceptions aren't the rule. Writing for young adults defies this description. You'll find books like Cecily von Ziegesar's *Gossip Girl* series sharing a bookshelf with M.T. Anderson's acclaimed literary novel *The Astonishing Life of Octavian Nothing, Traitor to the Nation*. Do such diverse books have anything in common? Is YA literature even a genre?

In 2006 there was a heated debate on author Malcolm Gladwell's blog about this very subject. In the course of an entry about plagiarism, Gladwell made the following comment: "This is teen literature.

It's genre fiction. These are novels based upon novels based upon novels ...

Needless to say, his opinion sparked much controversy and quite a few scathing responses. Numerous people pointed out that Gladwell's statement reflected his own ignorance of the scope and quality of books available for teens today, and that teen literature, in fact, encompasses *all* genres. Which is true. You'll find romance, science fiction, fantasy, mysteries, literary fiction, nonfiction, horror ...

According to the *The New Oxford American Dictionary*, the word *genre* means "a particular kind or style of art or literature." Does teen literature fit this definition? If it's not a genre, what's the glue that holds it together as a category?

The one defining characteristic of YA literature is its audience. Young adult books are written for or marketed to teens.

That's it.

Take almost any other element and try to use it to define the whole and you will find it falls short. Do YA books always feature teen protagonists? Most of the time, but when you look at books like Nancy Farmer's *The House of the Scorpion* and Markus Zusak's *The Book Thief*, you'll find lead characters of all ages. How about style? Aren't books for teens shorter, with fewer descriptive passages than adult books? Not always. Just look at Stephenie Meyer's rich and haunting *Twilight* series. How about modern-day relevance? Don't books for teens need to reflect their world? Many of them do, but there are also plenty of books written for young adults that qualify as historical fiction or take place in fantastical lands with no relationship to our own world whatsoever.

Even the definition of YA literature as "books written for teens" can be questioned. It's becoming increasingly common for books to be published for the adult audience in one country and marketed for the teen audience in another. If the author's intention was to write a book for adults, can we still classify it as YA literature if it gets marketed that way?

Young adult books are often referred to as coming-of-age literature, and many novels that are now regarded as YA classics, such as Robert Cormier's terrific novel *The Chocolate War*, actually began as adult novels that publishers couldn't find a niche for in the adult marketplace.

It's my belief that the only way to define YA literature is to continually go back to its audience and to allow for exceptions to every rule. Teens read books of all kinds, and that's a great thing. But YA literature is a category of books that deliberately appeals to the twelve-through eighteen-year-old age group. Do eleven-year-olds read teen novels? Of course. How about thirty-three-year-olds? You bet. But these are secondary audiences rather than the primary audience, and when a writer decides to write a YA novel, these are not the audiences that will shape the choices he makes.

Still confused?

If you really want to see how YA literature is defined, visit your local bookstore or spend time in the teen section at your library. Which books are included? If you were a teenager today, what would you find on the shelves? Take out as many books as you have time to read and see what they're like. Pay attention to every detail, from formatting and page count to characters and plot. What do they have in common? How are they different?

The very best way to understand literature of any kind is to read broadly. In fact, this is my number one, most important piece of advice for all writers. If you want to succeed, read!

DO YOU read BOOKS WRITTEN SPECIFICALLY FOR TEENS? WHY OR WHY NOT?

Long, age 17, California: Yes, and no. Novels and stories about young people tend to be more dynamic and in many ways universal. Adult situated books are entertaining if written well, but I will generally want to read something that will relate to me on a more personal level and give me insight, meaning, and substance. J.D. Salinger once said, "I almost always write about very young people." which explains it all, frankly.

Lindsay, age 12, Maine: No. I just read any book that sounds or looks interesting.

Jessica, age 18, Washington: I read teen-targeted books on a regular basis. There was a long while during my teenage years when I stopped reading them all together. Only in the last few years have there been so many fabulous, realistic books—and that's just what I love.

Destiny, age 15, New Mexico: Yes, because I understand them more than the ones for adults.

Kyle, age 14, California: Yes. They are written well and have exciting stories.

Hannah, age 15, New Mexico: I read teen books occasionally. All teen books seem to be the same to me. They all have similar themes and plots. And it is rare when a teen book comes out that I like.

Stephanie, age 17, Florida: I read tons of books classified in the YA category. In fact, most of the books I read are from there. The reason I do read them is because they're more fresh and realistic than adult novels. Most adult novels that I've seen center around sex and descriptions of said event that I truly don't care about. In YA books, they'll mention it but don't dwell over it. The YA novels give a different perspective to things than adult genres. It's the view and idea of someone who doesn't know all the answers and isn't going to. YA books to me are about finding yourself, ideas, and realizing, *no, we don't have the answers, just more questions and a whole lot of problems to solve along the way.*

WRITING WITH YOUR AUDIENCE IN MIND

So does all this confusion mean we can't write books for teens with any guidelines or principles in mind? Of course not. Even though books for teenagers vary widely, there are certain things they're *not*. For example, a toddler's picture book is clearly not intended as YA literature. An early chapter book with simple phrases that takes place in an elementary school is not meant to be YA literature. A book written for adults with long-winded passages about marriage and raising children is also not YA literature, although some young adults might choose to read any of these choices.

Young adult literature keeps its audience in mind, which means the books are generally (but not always) shorter than most adult books and longer than most books for elementary-age readers. Although manga (Japanese comics) and graphic novels are becoming very popular, most YA books don't have pictures to accompany the text. Language is usually sharp, and many people comment that the pace of YA books is quick, reflecting the pace of life for so many teens. Of course, there are always exceptions, but generally you want to keep your teen reader turning the pages before she gets distracted by the hundreds of things competing for her attention.

One way to do this is to feature a teen protagonist. While there are certainly YA novels that choose not to for one reason or another, the vast majority of teen literature shares this feature. Creating a teen protagonist allows your reader to relate to the character, perhaps even sharing certain characteristics or life experiences in common with him. The character can explore the world from a teenager's perspective.

Keeping this perspective in mind, you'll want to make choices about what material to present to your audience. Sometimes this might seem clear-cut, like not choosing life experiences your teen protagonist wouldn't have had yet; but other times it's not so clear-cut or might be defined by the novel itself. For example, parenthood might be a life experience you would relegate to adult novels, but Angela Johnson writes beautifully about teen fatherhood in her award-winning novel *The First Part Last*. Standing trial might seem like another subject best left for adults, but Walter Dean Myers's powerful novel *Monster* uses the trial of the main character to question the reader's understanding of legal vs. moral responsibility.

The world of YA literature is wide open to explore almost any subject as long as that exploration is consistent with the character you create and the circumstances that character finds herself in. Later on in Shop Class we'll discuss whether certain topics or words ought to be off-limits, but for the most part, writing for teens is about examining the world we live in, the choices we make as human beings, and the consequences of our actions.

Homework:

Homework from homeroom? I know, I know. But this is an easy assignment.

The best way to define YA literature is to see what's out there. Visit your local library and/or bookstore and study the shelves. If there's a separate section for teens (twelve to eighteen years old) and middle-grade readers (eight to twelve years old), try to determine what makes a book more suitable for one category than the other. Are there books that could fit into either one? As you peruse the shelves, try to figure out which characteristics of various titles seem tailored to the intended audience. Ask the librarian or bookseller which titles are most popular with teenagers. Then stroll over to the adult fiction shelves. How do the books appear the same? How do they seem different?

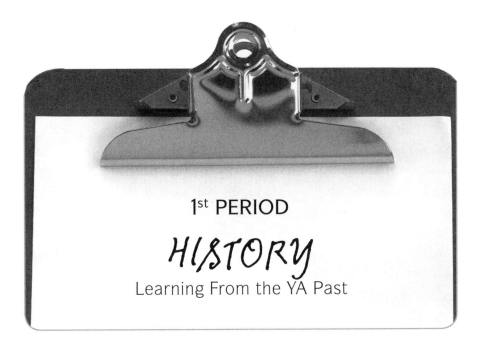

1st PERIOD

HISTORY

Learning From the YA Past

I'll confess, I've never been a history buff. For years I found history dull and could never retain the names and dates I'd memorized once the test was taken. It was as if my brain categorized that information as unnecessary and discarded it. It wasn't until I discovered biographies that history came alive. Finally, I could read about real people with fascinating lives, and the dates took on meaning. Armed with a form of history I loved to explore, I began to see how the past shaped the world we live in, and how it points to the future.

As you uncover the history of YA literature you'll begin to see how the stories you create have been influenced by the books published in the past decades and how the experiences of the authors, publishers, librarians, and booksellers who have promoted literature for young adults have paved the way for the books that are emerging today. You'll also get a fascinating glimpse into the ever-changing history of young people in the world, and maybe even some inkling as to what the future of books for teens might hold.

So, when exactly did YA literature begin?

Would you be surprised if I said the answer is unclear? Probably not. I imagine that, by now, you're gaining a sense of this art form being as transitory and difficult to pin down as its audience. If I asked you to guess what the first YA book was, you might think of S.E. Hinton's *The Outsiders* or J.D. Salinger's *The Catcher in the Rye*. Maybe one of Judy Blume's novels would come to mind. Or perhaps you'd go back even further to classics like Alexander Dumas's *The Count of Monte Cristo* or William Golding's *Lord of the Flies*.

These would all be excellent guesses.

The truth is, the history of literature written for young adults has a murky beginning that's complicated by the various definitions of terms like "adolescents," "teenagers," and "young adults," all of which have been used interchangeably at some points in history and been considered vastly different at other points.

According to *The New Oxford American Dictionary*, these words have the following meanings:

> adolescent (adj.): between childhood and maturity (n.)
> an adolescent person
>
> teenager (n.): a person in his or her teens
>
> teens (n.): the years of a person's age from thirteen
> to nineteen

Psychologist Erik Erikson, known for his research into the development of identity, defined a young adult as a person who is between the ages of nineteen and forty (*Childhood and Society*, 1950), but in literature we use this term to define books written for those between the ages of twelve and eighteen. With so much confusion over what exactly a young adult is, it's no wonder YA literature is hard to define!

The roles youth have played in the world, and the lines between childhood and adulthood, have shifted greatly over the centuries. Although our society tends to think of teenagers as being closer to children, this has not always been the prevailing attitude. People in their teens have been pharaohs, Roman emperors, kings, queens, sports champions, musicians, poets, best-selling authors, soldiers, parents, bohemians, and martyrs. At different times in the past, the period between youth and adulthood was nonexistent. People went directly from being children to taking on adult roles. Many times, these adult roles intruded into childhood, forcing children to work demanding and dangerous jobs.

In the past, many cultures held (and some still hold) coming-of-age ceremonies where the line between youth and adulthood is definitively marked for all to see, but in our society, the path to adulthood is not usually as clear. When exactly is a person grown up? For Americans, the idea of adolescence has evolved over the years.

Would it surprise you to know that in 1900 only 6 percent of seventeen-year-olds earned high school diplomas? (*Teenagers: An American History*, Grace Palladino, pg. xv) Back then, attending high school was not something young people took for granted. Most adolescents were responsible for helping their families on farms or in skilled trades. It wasn't until the Great Depression forced so many young people out of work and, consequently, out of their homes, that the government stepped in to make a high school education accessible to more than just the wealthy elite.

This shift away from disparate jobs to mass education allowed adolescents to take on an identity as a group, and people began to look at them differently. Young people now had more opportunity to relate to each other, and they gradually began to define themselves through their music, fashion, and beliefs. Often their definitions conflicted directly with adult attempts to impose more traditional values on them.

The tension between adult values and those of adolescents was certainly not a new thing in terms of world history—one need look no further than nineteenth-century France when so many of the impoverished artists included in the Bohemian subculture were young people who lived their nontraditional lifestyles in sharp opposition to their parents' wishes. But in America, this growing group would gain added attention and power as marketers slowly realized the economic value of reaching out to them. In fact, it was marketers who first used the term teenagers, beginning as "teeners," then "teensters," and finally becoming "teenagers" in 1941 (Palladino, pg. 52). Targeting adolescents with advertising was not new, but defining them as teenagers and viewing them as more than potential adults waiting to fill prescribed roles took some getting used to.

Teens and adults clashed about their choice of music and dress as the swing-loving bobby-soxers of the 1930s turned into the soldiers and V-girls of the 1940s, the rebellious rock-and-roll fanatics of the 1950s, and the long-haired hippies of the 1960s. As high school educations moved from being elite to commonplace, one thing was becoming quite clear: Young people were a powerful group who didn't intend to mimic their elders.

As teenagers took on their own group definitions, literature meant to address their specific needs and desires had a chance to catch on. Examples of books being written for young people can be found as early as the 1800s with books like Thomas Hughes's *Tom Brown's School Days* and Robert Louis Stevenson's *Treasure Island* gaining enormous success, but it wasn't until the 1940s that novels like Maureen Daly's *Seventeenth Summer*—often cited as the first book written in an authentic first-person teenage voice—and Betty Cavanna's *Going on Sixteen* paved the way for what would become YA literature. Even then, it wasn't until the 1950s that publishers and librarians first began to take this literature seriously.

You can see this evolution in the history of the Young Adult Library Services Association (YALSA). According to its Web site (www.ala.org/yalsa), the Young Adult Services Division, as it was originally known, was formally established in June of 1957. This marked a splitting of the Association of Young People's Librarians, which was established in 1941, into the Children's Library Association and the Young Adult Services Division. Their mission was to "advocate, promote, and strengthen service to young adults as part of the continuum of total library service."

One of the functions the Young Adult Services Division retained from the original Association of Young People's Librarians was the compiling of the annual Best Books for Young Adults list, which began in 1952 and was known throughout the years as "Interesting Books" and "Significant Adult Books for Teens" before finally ending up as the list we know today.

I mention these changes and the dates associated with them as a reflection of the way literature for teens has grown over the years. What began as a market where adult books might find popularity among teenagers has gradually developed into something much more deliberate.

This burgeoning interest in literature for teenagers took a giant leap forward when government money became available to libraries in the 1960s under Lyndon Johnson's presidency. Johnson saw education as a central part of fostering the American Dream, and libraries used this funding, in part, to create YA sections and buy the books that would populate these shelves. Not coincidentally, it was around this same time period that groundbreaking books like S.E. Hinton's *The Outsiders* and Paul Zindel's *The Pigman* burst onto the scene and expanded the boundaries of what could be included in teen fiction.

As the teens of the 1930s, 1940s, and 1950s grew up, they began to write books about their own experiences as teenagers. Rather than reflecting the view of teenagers as mini-adults, waiting to obediently take on their roles as homemakers and workers, they brought to the literature they created the same openness and honesty they'd fought hard for over the decades. By the 1970s books for teens had taken on a new realism that reflected the social issues of the time. Books like *Go Ask Alice*, which dealt with teen pregnancy, Judy Blume's *Forever*, which spoke frankly about sex and birth control, and John Donovan's *I'll Get There, It Better Be Worth the Trip*, which deals with homosexuality, didn't pull any punches in their portrayal of teenagers and the tough choices they face as they mature.

This tendency to focus on harsh realities was both a blessing and a curse for YA literature. The books from this time period broke down boundaries of acceptable subject matter and language, and they gave teens a voice of their own, but many of them also gave rise to the stigma of teen books as "problem novels"—underdeveloped stories, didactic in nature, that focused on issues rather than literary merit. Despite how varied literature for teens is today, the perception remains among many people that YA literature is somehow subpar.

Nothing could be farther from the truth.

If the pendulum swung too far toward didacticism in the 1970s, 1980s, and 1990s, it was probably because there were so many barriers to break down—barriers that didn't exist to the same degree in adult literature. Teenagers as a group had only just begun to define themselves, and this sense of shifting identity is evident in the books written for and by them. Multiculturalism and acceptance of other sexual orientations also were just beginning to gain a foothold in our country; the irony is that the same teens who historically have been so instrumental in bringing about change in these areas are also the very same group that adults often try hardest to shelter.

Nowhere is this more evident than in the banning of YA books that push the boundaries of what's culturally acceptable. YA writers have always had to fight hard to write what they see as true, even if that truth is uncomfortable, and this was every bit the case when the "problem novel" reached its zenith. Unfortunately, this meant that by the 1990s many librarians and booksellers were tolling the death knell for teen literature. Add to this the fact that in the 1980s not only had the percentage of teenagers in America declined, but library funding had been cut by the Reagan administration, and it's no surprise that teen bookshelves and teen specialists were the first to disappear in many libraries across the country.

We can thank two groups for the survival of YA books. First, the authors who consistently wrote amazing, literary novels through all of these decades, defying the negative stereotypes of books for teenagers, and second, the librarians, editors, and booksellers who championed these novels even when others were ready to throw in the towel. It's thanks to them that a field once thought to be on the brink of collapse has become a thriving, vital part of global literature.

Now, many people are saying that we've arrived at a new golden age for YA literature. Over the last two decades we've seen the population of teenagers in America grow tremendously and, by some statistics, that growth won't peak until 2010. We've seen the advent of the YA paperback, which made teen books affordable to their audience and easily distributed, and we've seen the emergence of graphic novels and manga as creative and popular choices for teens. Multicultural books have moved from being nearly nonexistent to being sought after, and more and more books are being written from perspectives other than white, middle class, or wealthy teens. In 1999 the Young Adult Services Division of the American Library Association established the first Michael L. Printz awards to honor literary excellence in books written for twelve- through eighteen-year-olds, so now it's much easier for excellent teen novels to gain the recognition and attention they deserve.

This is an exciting time to be a writer for teenagers. Authors today have fewer restrictions and more recognition than ever before, and with the prevalence of the Internet we have increasing opportunities to market our books directly to our audience. Though you may not always like what they have to say, rap and hip-hop artists have given teens an ear for rhythm and wordplay, and social networking sites like MySpace have given teen authors a fun, accessible image.

Are there still challenges? Definitely. Did you know that the Teen Choice Awards recognize just about every form of entertainment other than books? They give out awards for TV, movies, sports, fashion, and music, but I suspect if anyone suggested they include a "Best

Book" category the idea would never be taken seriously. Why is that? The answer to this question is something that writers for young adults should consider. How do teenagers today view books, and are we doing all we can to keep them reading?

Hopefully the answer is yes, and the books we write today will be part of tomorrow's history—a history other writers will draw on as inspiration for the work they will do in the future.

Teen Panel

WHY DO YOU THINK THE TEEN CHOICE AWARDS DON'T INCLUDE A CATEGORY FOR BEST TEEN NOVEL? DO YOU CONSIDER BOOKS A FORM OF ENTERTAINMENT?

Erin, age 16, Idaho: The Teen Choice Awards are mostly about what's hot at the moment. They're not really about a truly brilliant performance or screenplay, etc.—more about what song is catchy and what comedian appeals to certain teens' senses of humor. Books are all about quality, and no offense, but I don't believe the Teen Choice Awards really are. Books are definitely a form of entertainment! Give me a book over TV or movies any day.

Jermaine, age 16, New Mexico: I think a good book is a form of entertainment. Most teens don't read because they don't know if the book will be interesting or not. Therefore, very few teens read outside of school, which is why books are not included in the awards.

Ilana, age 17, Florida: I most definitely consider books a form of entertainment. It's my main entertainment. I just don't know how many teens there are out there like me. We're a minority, us bibliophiles. I think that, like most award shows, Teen Choice is run by adults and their idea of what interests us is based on stereotypes. Teen girls are stereotyped to be interested in hair, makeup, boys, and simplified non-intelligent forms of entertainment. Teen boys are often stereotyped as being interested in sex, sports, and video games. Also not thought of as vessels for intelligent entertainment.

Mercedes, age 15, New Mexico: I consider them a form of entertainment, but only if it is leisure reading, not an assignment. Best Teen Novel might not be a category because the majority of American teens don't associate reading with entertainment.

Lacey, age 16, Michigan: Pop culture, for the majority, has become as cheap and easy as fast food. Teens want to sit down, have a laugh, stand up thirty minutes later and move on with their lives. Books seem too time consuming to most youth.

Aarika, age 17, California: Teens nowadays barely read for leisure, which is a shame, so there is hardly a call for best teen novel when teenagers are more concerned with "teen hottie." I personally consider books a great form of entertainment and a better way to spend time than wasting away in front of the TV.

Homework:

Remember the most important piece of advice I gave you at the beginning of this book? Read, read, and read some more? Well, here's a chance to put it into practice. By reading books published since novels first began to be written and marketed deliberately for teens, you'll not only gain a better understanding of how YA books evolved, you'll have a chance to read some classics in the genre.

I've compiled a list of several books from each decade. These aren't necessarily the most literary or acclaimed books; instead, they've been chosen to give you a representative feel for what was being published at the time. For example, *Slumber Party* by Christopher Pike is one of many horror novels that took off during the series craze of the 1980s. *Oh My Goddess! 1-555-GODDESS* by Kosuke Fujishima is one of many possible examples of manga, which has been gaining popularity in the United States since the 1990s.

Read as few or as many of these books as you have time for. This assignment isn't meant to scare you—I know your life is busy! In fact, I'm hoping this list will serve as an easy reference tool, cutting down on the time it takes you to establish your YA reading list. So, don't stress yourself trying to read them all, but whenever you have a chance, choose a title and read it with a critical and historical eye. (I had good luck finding many of the older books on Amazon.com, at used bookstores, and through library book sales.)

1940s: *Seventeenth Summer* by Maureen Daly
(Dodd, Mead, 1942)

Going on Sixteen by Betty Cavanna
(Westminster Press, 1946)

1950s: *The Sea Gulls Woke Me* by Mary Stolz
(Harper, 1951)

The Catcher in the Rye by J.D. Salinger
(Little, Brown, 1951)

Sorority Girl by Anne Emery
(Westminster Press, 1952)

A Separate Peace by John Knowles
(Secker & Warburg, 1959)

1960s: *The Outsiders* by S.E. Hinton
(Viking Press, 1967)

The Pigman by Paul Zindel
(Harper & Row, 1968)

Writing & Selling the *YA novel*

The Left Hand of Darkness by Ursula K. Le Guin
(Walker, 1969)

1970s: *Are You There God? It's Me, Margaret*
by Judy Blume (Bradbury Press, 1970)

Go Ask Alice by Anonymous
(Prentice Hall, 1971)

Dinky Hocker Shoots Smack by M.E. Kerr
(Harper & Row, 1972)

The Chocolate War by Robert Cormier
(Pantheon Books, 1974)

1980s: *Annie on My Mind* by Nancy Garden
(Farrar, Straus and Giroux, 1982)

The Divorce Express by Paula Danziger
(Delacorte Press, 1982)

Running Loose by Chris Crutcher
(Greenwillow Books, 1983)

Slumber Party by Christopher Pike
(Scholastic, 1985)

Weetzie Bat by Francesca Lia Block
(Harper & Row, 1989)

1990s: *Maniac Magee* by Jerry Spinelli
(Little, Brown, 1990)

Oh My Goddess! 1-555-GODDESS by Kosuke Fujishima
(Dark Horse, 1995)

Rats Saw God by Rob Thomas
(Simon & Schuster, 1996)

Speak by Laurie Halse Anderson
(Farrar, Straus and Giroux, 1999)

2000s: *The Sisterhood of the Traveling Pants*
by Ann Brashares (Delacorte Press, 2001)

The First Part Last by Angela Johnson
(Simon & Schuster, 2003)

Twilight by Stephenie Meyer
(Little, Brown 2005)

The Book Thief by Markus Zusak
(Alfred A. Knopf, 2006)

American Born Chinese by Gene Luen Yang
(First Second, 2006)

2nd PERIOD

gym

Tossing Around—and Running With—Ideas

So, now you know what YA novels are and how they've evolved. We've discussed motivation, and you've read widely from books spanning many decades. It's time to start writing.

Perhaps this is the moment you've been waiting for. You're ready. You're pumped. Like an athlete who is prepared to go the distance, you've got the enthusiasm and the drive. But what you may not have yet is an idea. It's difficult to imagine yourself running up the art museum steps in the *Rocky* montage if you don't have the big fight scheduled. Finding the right idea is the key to beginning your YA novel.

So where, exactly, do ideas come from? How can you find ideas that teenagers will enjoy? The answer to this question is both simple and complex.

Ideas for your teen novel can come from anywhere. That's the simple answer. But the real question is: Where do *good* ideas come from? How can you tell the difference between an idea that will sizzle and one that will never heat up? Are there unique sources for ideas that will appeal to the teen marketplace?

Whether you loved or hated gym class in school, this version of gym will be nothing like what you were used to. In this gym class, the muscle we'll be working on is your brain. Priming your creative muscle is hard work, so let's get some blood flowing with a few mental calisthenics.

WHERE DO IDEAS COME FROM?

A good workout starts out slow, so let's begin with the easy stuff. Where can you find ideas for your novel? Since you're writing for teens are you limited to MTV, movies, TV, and the mall?

Absolutely not.

Ideas can come from so many places they'd be impossible to count, and finding ideas for a teen novel is no different than finding ideas for an adult novel. Sure, you might want to focus more on school and less on the workplace, but remember that teens live in the exact same world that adults live in, and that world is rich with story potential.

In fact, our world is overflowing with stories. Whether they come in the form of movies, books, TV shows, or song lyrics, there are stories swirling around us prett much all the time. Obviously we can't use them in the exact same forms that we find them, but we can allow them to inspire us.

Many authors are inspired by music, and I include myself in that group. Listening to music makes me want to capture the same raw emotion I hear through the lyrics and melody, only in a different form. When I find myself hitting a creative wall, I put on a good CD and let my mind wander. Do you have to listen to the same music that's popular with teens? At times that might be helpful, but generally the idea is for you to be inspired, so it's more important that the music move *you*, rather than reflecting your target audience.

There are also times when a director's commentary on a DVD has sparked an idea for a book. Learning about the creative process other artists go through, even if they aren't in the same field, can inspire you to look at your own work from a different angle. Hearing how a screenwriter or director stepped outside of the conventional forms found in film can prompt you to step out of the creative box that might be holding you back. Again, you need not confine yourself to teen movies, but in this case, listening to how these artists connect to their teen audiences just might inspire you to connect with yours.

I've also been inspired by other books. Reading a great book can get me so excited that suddenly my mind is overflowing with ideas. Where once my imaginative muscles might have felt stiff and sore, after reading a great book, they're ready to work out. It's the literary equivalent of a cup of coffee or a protein bar. Great books generate enthusiasm, and enthusiasm sparks ideas. Read all kinds of books, and allow them to get you excited. Excitement works like a furnace for ideas, or at least idea receptivity. When you're excited, your mind opens to every possible form an idea might take. You look at the world around you in a new way, and this is exactly what it takes to find great stories.

If you're looking for ideas, watch the world around you and take note of interesting people, places, or events. Read books, newspapers, and magazines. Reality can be a wonderful source for fiction. The very first YA novel I ever attempted was inspired by a true story in *Newsweek* about teens in a small town who started a gay/straight student alliance. The teens captured my imagination, and I wanted to know more about their lives: What had brought them to that point, and what would happen to them afterwards? I explored those possibilities as I wrote my book (using fictional characters and plot, of course). Although that novel didn't sell, it's still a story I'm proud of. It's a 250-page novel that wouldn't have existed without that one-page article.

When you watch the world around you, keep an eye out for conflict and tension. Part of what appealed to me about that particular news story was that the teens were meeting with resistance from the school board and people in their town. This intrigued me. I wanted to know how they would handle the opposition and how the situation would get resolved. Conflict makes for great stories, and although we wish it didn't exist, it's everywhere. When you read about conflict, see it on TV, or even if you witness it firsthand, ask yourself if there's a book somewhere in there that you'd be interested in writing. Does the real-life situation make you curious, angry, sad, or joyful enough that you'd want to capture those same emotions in a novel?

Patricia McCormick did a fabulous job of turning conflict into a powerful, emotional story with her novel *Sold*, which is about a girl from Nepal who is sold into prostitution. A chance meeting with a photographer working undercover brought the issue of girls in brothels to McCormick's attention. She describes on her Web site how she knew immediately that she wanted to try and tell this story from a single girl's point of view. The resulting book received a National Book Award nomination.

What's happening in the world that's of interest to *you*? What do you think would interest teens? Ask yourself how a teenager might fit into a story that catches your eye. One of the unique aspects of writing for young adults is that the teenage point of view is seldom portrayed in the media when it comes to world events. We most often hear from adults, and occasionally someone might interview a small child, but generally teens are overlooked. When we take the time to explore their view of the world, the results are almost always fascinating.

One word of caution, though: Just because you intend to write for teens doesn't mean you should ignore anything you perceive as being outside the teen perspective. When it comes to finding ideas, be open to everything. Even situations that seem adult can be explored from a young person's point of view. Do politics interest you? Maybe your character is a summer intern at the United States Capitol. Are you a huge fan of NASCAR? Perhaps your character is the child of one of the drivers. How does he feel about his parent's risky profession?

Persepolis by Marjane Satrapi is a great example of a graphic novel that explores adult situations from the perspective of first a child, and then a teen. This story is the memoir of a woman who grew up in Iran during the Islamic Revolution. Throughout the course of the book we witness acts of war and experience the hardships of political repression through Marjane's young eyes. The result is a book that brings history to life in a way that a strictly adult novel could not.

Marjane Satrapi not only doesn't hesitate to explore adult issues from a young person's perspective, she also does something we can all do at any time. She delves into her memories. I know what you're thinking: "But I didn't grow up during the Islamic Revolution! My life is not nearly that interesting."

Isn't it?

Who can say what might be fascinating to someone who hasn't experienced it? And unless you're writing a memoir, you don't need to use your memories in a literal manner. Use them to spark ideas instead. Choose an event from your own teenage years and ask yourself why it stands out in your mind. Is there a strong emotion attached to it? If so, maybe that's an emotion you'd want to explore at greater length. Do you remember a specific situation that was dangerous, humorous, or sad? How might you update it for today's teens? Or maybe you'd rather include it in a historical fiction novel. The opportunities are endless, so take out those old journals and diaries.

Be sure to dig out your photo albums, too. Photographs remind us of people and places we might otherwise have forgotten. They are rich in details and expression. Even when the photos aren't yours, they can still be sources of inspiration. I've always loved to stare into the eyes of strangers in photographs and wonder about their stories. What were they like? How did their lives turn out? Were they happy? Studying the clues a photo offers can spark even more ideas. Where is the person? Who else is in the picture? What are the people doing? Is there anything interesting happening in the background? Photographs are everywhere, so take time to really look at them.

ASKING QUESTIONS

Starting to work up a sweat yet? Be sure to take a breather. Taking time out is as important when you're searching for ideas as it is during a workout. The writing process can't be rushed. In fact, one of the best ways to generate ideas is simply to sit still and observe the world. Writers need time to explore every possible idea that occurs to them. One way to do this is through asking questions.

Asking questions of everything you see is essential because in any given situation, the right question might unlock the perfect story. As writers, we are constantly exploring the world. We ask ourselves what it would be like to live as someone else. What would that person do, say, and think? Ask questions as you watch a teen on the subway. What would it be like to be him or her? When you see an interesting house, ask yourself who lives there. If you see a large family, take time to wonder what it might be like to be one of many children. Or if you already know the answer to that question, ask yourself what it would be like to be an only child. As you delve into this process, you'll find that each question will lead to another until eventually a particular line of questions will capture your attention so much that you don't want to abandon it. When the questions seem endless, there's a good chance you've found your story.

Realistic questions aren't the only ones that can spark ideas. A different type of question you might use is the "What if " question. Start a question with "What if" and then fill in the blank. For example, you might ask yourself, "What if I was the child of an immigrant family?" or "What if the world entered a new ice age?" or "What if we could travel back in time?" While this technique works well for realistic situations, it's also great for generating ideas outside the familiar realm. I especially recommend it if you're searching for teen fantasy or science fiction ideas. By asking ourselves "What if" questions, we can twist reality until it becomes unrecognizable.

If you like a particular question and its answer, be sure to follow it through until you run out of questions. For example, you might start with a question like this: What if I lived on a planet almost exactly like this one, only in a different galaxy? Then you could add: What if my family was one of the first to colonize this planet and we did so just before a nuclear holocaust on Earth, so now we are forgotten? Continue on to: What if there were no other teenagers and I couldn't stand my parents?

Let each question spark the next question. You might even combine questioning techniques so you can see a story from every angle. Maybe the teen who hates his family is somehow different from them, so although others in the group tolerate him, he's not taken seriously in this harsh environment. Ask yourself what it might be like to be different. How would he prove himself to others? What kind of a struggle might he and his family have gone through in order to make it to the planet in the first place? How did the teen feel about leaving Earth? Now that they're stranded, does he feel vindicated or foolish? How does he handle his emotions?

By starting with a "What if" question, you can arrive at an idea that might lead you to a character. What began as a scenario has now reached the point where human emotions are involved, and those emotions will lead to actions that will define the person in your mind. Now he's no longer a teenage placeholder, he's a boy with intense struggles who must deal with extreme isolation. As you ask yourself *how* he does this, and *why* he does this, your answers will shape his character until soon, he just might become unforgettable.

MEMORIES

When an idea sticks in your mind, there's usually a reason. W.H. Auden said, "Some books are undeservedly forgotten; none are undeservedly remembered." The same could be said for people, places, and events. Don't be afraid to delve into your own memories or let the memoirs of others inspire you. Many writers get hung up on the idea that every facet of a story must come from their own imaginations, but every one of us draws from real life all the time. I find biographies to be excellent idea generators, and the details they reveal about a particular time and place can be helpful in creating a setting.

Interviews are also excellent ways of learning about the past or finding out key information. Ask people questions about their past and present. Maybe your neighbor was one of those first "teenagers" we learned about in Homeroom. Find out what it was like to live through World War II, then let those memories suggest possible story ideas. Even if you don't end up using the actual events the person describes in a book, you might get an idea based on the emotions involved. Hearing the true account of someone's first love or last goodbye might spark a novel full of romance or pathos. Just be sure to make the story your own.

Interviews aren't relegated to the elderly, either! Try interviewing teens. Ask them about their lives. What kind of school do they go to? What are their daily struggles? What do they want to be when they grow up? What kind of books do they like to read? Or you could interview school principals. What do they see happening in the halls from day to day? Which kids break their hearts and which ones drive them crazy?

Questions work so well as idea-generating tools in part because they allow us to reach out to the world around us. Whether that takes the form of imagination, empathy, or fact gathering, when we're asking questions we're engaged with reality—what it is, what we wish it were, and what it could be. Engaging in the world is essential for any writer. The more you notice and experience, the more extensive your palette of ideas.

Emily, age 17, California: I think I would definitely have that author focus more on family and heritage. In the books I read, there isn't enough of home and family. I would have that author write about my heritage or maybe my mother's heritage (she is adopted so we don't really know) or even the divorce in my family. I feel like it needs to be explored more.

Esli, age 15, New Mexico: I wouldn't give an author an idea; I would tell this author to help me write my own story because this way I can add details the author may not know, which would make the book better.

Natasha, age 15, Maine: A struggle because of an injury during a sports season.

Sara-Elizabeth, age 12, New York: I would probably give an author something about animal rescue because not many people really write things that go straight to the ASPCA and more people should save animals.

James, age 12, New Mexico: A story about cars and racing. I love Ford Mustangs. I take them apart and put them together. You can put any Mustang in front of me and I can tell you what kind it is, what size of engine, and a lot of things.

John, age 16, Michigan: A story idea I would give would be about my parents' divorce and how to deal with it. I would suggest this idea because this was something that had a big impact on my life and it is something that teens are going through more and more.

Writing & Selling the *YA novel*

HOW TO CHOOSE THE BEST IDEA

By now your brain should be wide awake, ready for action. It's time for the real workout to begin. Anyone can warm up, but only true athletes run the race to the finish line. What's the finish line for a writer? It's moving from having many potential story ideas to choosing *one* and turning it into a book. Can you reach the finish line with your writing? Absolutely. The first step is choosing the best idea to pursue.

So, how do you find the one idea you want to write your book about? This process is twofold. You not only have to find the idea that works best for you; it also has to be the right time for that idea. Sometimes, an idea that seems only so-so at the present might come back strong a year or two later. Perhaps events in your own life might shift in a way that makes a story about loss or pain or joy suddenly more compelling. I know many authors who keep idea files for just this reason. They jot down their story ideas on index cards and then store them away. This way they can go back to an old idea at any time; an idea is never lost.

Personally, I let my subconscious do the sifting for me. When an idea is compelling enough that it won't leave me alone—when I come back to it again and again and again—that's a story I'll pursue. Some ideas might stick around for years before I'm ready to write them. Others force their way forward fairly quickly.

The "sticky" factor is extremely important in determining which idea to turn into a novel. Writing a book can take months or even years, so it's important that the idea you choose can hold your interest for that amount of time. It needs to be something you deeply care about rather than something that seems good at the moment.

A large part of this "stickiness" will be how you feel about your main character. We'll talk more about characters next period, but for now I'd like to mention that idea generating is not just about coming up with plots. This is a common misconception among beginning writers who equate a fabulous idea with the next great plot device. In reality, ideas can come in the form of characters as well as plots, and it's often the characters who are the most apt to grab us and not let go.

One thing I learned during my time in publishing is that no matter how unique you think your idea is, chances are someone else has thought of a similar plot. I asked my editor about this when, just before *Fat Kid Rules the World* was to be published, another editor sent us a link to an Australian book called *Fat Boy Saves World*, by Ian Bone. I was shocked. How was it possible someone else had come up with a title so similar to my own? I panicked, but my editor did not. She told me that when a story comes from the heart, the way an author writes it and the characters she creates are what will make the book unique. I've kept this in mind ever since, focusing on characters and my own emotional involvement rather than depending on a clever plot device when choosing which ideas to pursue.

You also need to choose ideas that have meaning and relevance for you rather than ideas you perceive as marketable. Just as our perception of originality can be shattered by someone unexpectedly publishing a book with a similar title or plot, our perceptions of marketability can also change in an instant. Before the first *Harry Potter* was published, fantasy was waning, but afterwards it has seen an unprecedented surge in sales.

This is great for aspiring fantasy writers, right? Maybe you have only a marginal interest in fantasy but think you could produce a solid submission while the market is ripe. Unfortunately, you're not the only one who thinks this. Whenever a book in a given genre makes it big, there's always a corresponding surge in people wanting to write and submit similar books. So, although the market has increased, so has your competition.

Many aspiring authors don't realize how long the publishing process takes, and they assume they'll have time to write and submit a book before the market changes again. In reality, even if you are a very fast writer, the submission process can take many months or even years. If you've based your book on an idea of what will sell, chances are that will have changed by the time your novel is being considered by editors.

It's been said many times before, but it's worth saying again: *Write what you love!* When choosing an idea to pursue, banish all thoughts of marketability and focus on where you can invest the biggest piece of your soul. Which idea has personal relevance for you, and which idea do you think will have the most relevance to your teen readers? Which book would you write even if I told you right now that it would never sell to a publishing house?

That's the idea to choose.

ARTICLES VS. NOVELS

Hopefully, by now you're ready to cool down. This is the time to stand back, breathe deeply, and take one more hard look at the idea you've chosen. I believe passion should be foremost in your mind right now, but there are some practical considerations as well.

When I worked at Curtis Brown, Ltd., we often submitted nonfiction proposals to editors. One of the most common reasons editors gave for rejecting a proposal was the phrase, "This is an article, not a book." In other words, it's a catchy idea, but no one's going to want to read two or three hundred pages of it. Whether you're writing fiction or nonfiction, the "article test" is a good one to apply. Ask yourself what kind of depth an idea can inspire. What level of conflict is present? What might a character need to learn from beginning to end and which obstacles might she have to overcome? Is there enough substance to sustain a whole book?

It might be helpful at this point to determine what your motivation is for wanting to pursue a given idea. Are you driven by a true desire to tell the story or do you see the story as a vehicle to make a point? When it comes to books for teens, writers often want to teach or guide, and there's nothing wrong with that as long as the story comes first. Otherwise, you'll most likely find that your idea fizzles midway through. Could you read a two hundred-page lecture? Probably not, and neither will the average teen. If your motivation is primarily to instruct, perhaps there's another venue better suited to what you have to say.

In fact, choosing the right venue for an idea is as essential as coming up with a good idea in the first place. Certain ideas will, naturally, be better suited to certain styles of writing. I'll give you an example from my own experience.

One afternoon, my husband was relating a story about an event that happened in an NFL football Xbox game he'd been playing with a friend. He told me about the event as if it had been real, and it was only because of my prior knowledge of the game's existence that I knew he and his friend had not actually made the play he was telling me about. This sparked a "What if " question: What if in the future games become so common and so advanced that people cease to do anything real but still feel as if they have accomplished great things?

Based on this question, I extrapolated a scene where a group of teens discuss their accomplishments. Only at the end of the conversation would the reader realize the characters had never left their own living rooms. Their "great deeds" had, in fact, all taken place in virtual reality.

At first this idea seemed novel-worthy, but as I began to think about it, I wondered if it would really carry through for several hundred pages. Would I be able to maintain the illusion so the ending could be a surprise? How would my action and character development be limited because of my plot device? Was there a single character I could develop in a compelling way? How would that character change from beginning to end if the success of the story was dependent on the reader's discovery that the character had, in fact, been doing nothing?

As I looked at the elements involved, I realized that for me, this story idea would work best as a short story. It's clever, but clever doesn't sustain hundreds of pages. Characters do. An alternative would be to develop an interesting character who could fit into the predetermined plot, but that kind of plot-driven novel often seems forced. So, while compelling, this idea was a wrong fit for my next novel.

Figuring out which ideas are compelling and which ideas are merely clever can be one of the most difficult parts of your journey to becoming a published writer. As you gain experience, you will learn which forms of writing work best for you, and then you'll be able to decide which format most naturally suits both the idea *and* your writing style. This will save you countless hours of work and allow you to focus on the stories you can tell with passion and drive.

Homework: Find five possible ideas from any of the following sources: a newspaper, a magazine, a piece of music, an interview, a photograph, an advertisement, an over-heard conversation, a line of dialogue from a teen movie, a dream, your high school yearbook.

Write down each idea and beside it write the form(s) you think best suit the idea: nonfiction, short story, screenplay, fiction, play, poem. Ask yourself which ideas you are most drawn to and why. Do the best formats also fit your strengths as a writer? Which of the ideas (if any) could you see yourself sticking with the longest? Which one would you write even if you were guaranteed it would never get published?

 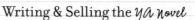

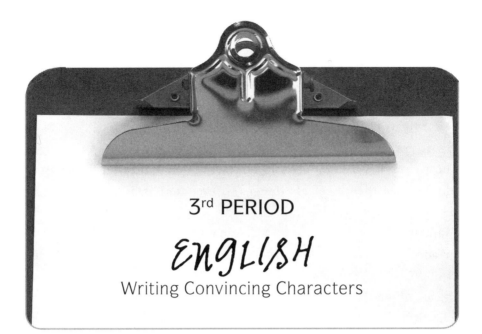

3rd PERIOD

ENGLISH

Writing Convincing Characters

As a teen, English was always my favorite class. I loved to read and already kept a journal, so the idea that I could get school credit for doing these things was almost too good to be true. I devoured every book the teachers assigned and fell in love with most of them—even the classics. If you'd asked me back then what made me love the books I read, I'm not sure I would've been able to answer. They didn't seem to have much in common. I read from every genre and loved most styles of writing. Like many teens, I was just as apt to pick up an adult novel as a teen novel, and my bookshelf was full of books like *Wuthering Heights* shelved side by side with the newest R.A. Salvatore fantasy novel.

Now as an adult I look at the books I've loved over the years and can see that they all share one thing in common: great characters. Whether it's Heathcliff or Drizzt Do'Urden, the characters hook me into a book and make me want to keep reading. It was the love of character that made English my favorite class year after year, and creating unique characters is now my favorite part of being an author. Ideas are wonderful, but they won't go very far without interesting, lovable, or infuriating characters to embody them.

In Nancy Lamb's *The Writer's Guide to Crafting Stories for Children*, she writes: "What happens to characters—how they suffer and celebrate, how they meet challenges, overcome obstacles and find redemption—is the heart and soul and spirit of story." This is true no matter who your audience is. Whether you're writing for teens, kids, or adults, creating memorable characters is what elevates an idea from a novelty to a story with substance that will draw us in and make us care about the outcome. If your audience invests in your characters, whether that investment comes in the form of love, hate, or morbid fascination, they'll keep turning the pages and following the story until the bitter end.

So what makes a good character? Why do some characters live while others fall flat? How can you create teen characters who are both believable and sympathetic? In this chapter we'll take a look at creating the characters who will bring your stories to life.

WHAT MAKES A CHARACTER?

Understanding character begins with understanding people. What makes them tick? How do we relate to others? How do people grow and change over the course of a lifetime? How are teenagers different from adults and children?

Every human being has certain attributes, but those attributes are always in flux. We have physical attributes such as eye color, hair color, age, weight, and height, as well as myriad other features that make us unique—large ears, a small nose, or exceptionally big feet.

Many of these physical traits will change as we grow and mature, and teen characters, especially, are in transition. Their bodies are growing, and this growth will have a vast array of consequences that will affect other attributes.

For example, physical changes such as puberty often lead to changes in personality, and personality traits are a big part of defining a character. Teens can be irritable, kind, stingy, open, rude, false, generous, conniving, hyper, morose, or curious, just to name a few. They are often many of these things simultaneously, and over the course of a lifetime each person will embody almost every personality trait there is.

Our personalities reveal themselves through our speech, actions, and body language. Every person has a unique way of talking, walking, sitting, eating, sleeping, and doing just about any activity you can think of. We all have habits and idiosyncrasies, but again, these habits don't stay the same forever. Consider how you acted when you were a teen. Do you ever look back and laugh at some of the ways you tried to seem grown up? Maybe you wore too much makeup or emulated your favorite pop star. Or maybe you look back and feel sad that you've lost some of the idealism you possessed when you were younger. Teens are often purposefully trying to shape their habits, looking to mold themselves into the people they'd like to become, and those imagined future selves might be rich and famous, or they might be saving the world. Or both!

Watching what a character does or does *not* do can reveal what she wants and help create a fuller sense of who she is both physically and emotionally. This is especially true when we reveal the reasons behind her actions. Although different people may appear to make similar decisions, our choices are based on our varied life experiences. When we reveal a character's history and inner life, in addition to showing his actions, we shed light on his motivations, attitudes, desires, and struggles, and this adds depth to our portrayal.

MAKING CHOICES

Do you have the feeling that all the attributes listed above still only scratch the surface of what defines a character? If so, you're right. Each character we create is a totally distinct person, and it's our job to reveal them to the world. But there's a wealth of information that can be conveyed about any human being, and teens are especially complex because they are still figuring out who they are and what roles they want to take in life. So how do we give the reader an accurate portrait?

We do it by making choices.

Part of what it means to be an author is deciding which information to convey to your reader and how to convey it. Writing isn't just about putting words on a page; it's about artistry. Like any artist, you'll need to make decisions about what to include or exclude in order to produce the most impact or the greatest beauty.

When it comes to character development, choices are essential. Obviously you can't describe every character trait—if you did, you'd fill entire volumes with description and there'd be no room for anything to actually *happen* in the story, nor would there be any artistry. Instead, choose which features best define your character; this description can be a mix of physical traits, personality, backstory, and character choices.

Perhaps the easiest way to think about this decision-making process is to imagine I've asked you to describe your best friend. If you tried to tell me everything about her, it would take forever because people are always changing, and just about the time you told me what your friend was like she'd have changed clothes, hairstyle, and attitude, and moved on to some new activity. So, instead of trying to tell me everything, you'd tell me the important things—the things I most needed to know to get an accurate picture of her.

You might tell me the basics of what she looks like, such as hair color and whether she was tall or short, skinny or full-figured. You might also include some characteristics that make her unique. Maybe you'd tell me her skin color or religious beliefs, or perhaps you'd mention her thin lips or large nose. But mostly, I imagine you'd tell me what kind of person she is, and you'd probably use examples of things your friend has done or said to convince me of your points.

> … and on top of everything else, she's brilliant. She was valedictorian of her graduating class and she got a scholarship to Yale.
>
> She's so funny. Every time we go out, she's the life of the party.

You might also tell me something of your friend's personal history to further illuminate her character.

> I love her, but she can be difficult to deal with. She's very temperamental, but I know it's because she had a tough life growing up with two alcoholic parents. Considering all she's been through, she's a real strong person. Once you're her friend she's fiercely loyal.
>
> Some people think she's shallow because she parties so much, but honestly, she's the most generous

> person I know. Her family was poor when she was young,
> so she has a strong desire to help needy children.

People are complex—we aren't easily summed up by one or two descriptions. Teen characters are no different. To reveal them, we must draw from a palette that includes every available trait, but we must also make choices about which traits most clearly define the person we're describing.

What we most need to know about a character is what makes him who he is and what will drive his actions. Many times, especially for teens, physical appearance plays a large part in this. An awkward teen will behave very differently from an effortlessly beautiful one. Not only will she make different choices, she will move differently through space. Race, sexuality, or family background can also affect our body language, our worldviews, and the decisions we make.

Each piece of the character puzzle is important, but every story will require different information to be revealed. For example, you might think race is an essential trait that an audience must know in order to "see" a character in their mind's eye, but Virginia Euwer Wolff, in her books *Make Lemonade* and *True Believer*, made a deliberate choice not to reveal the race of her characters. Wolff wanted readers to make the characters into whatever race they needed them to be. This is a risky choice that takes a lot of skill to pull off, but through her insights into the characters' hearts and minds, we're able to feel as if we know them even while we're missing a large piece of their physical description.

This is not only an example of an author making a choice, it's a choice that illustrates what's truly essential about defining character.

While physicality is important, in the end, it's what characters do and say that makes them real to a reader.

Think about the characters you create. What will your reader need to know to make them real? Do you allow for complexity? How does a character's physical appearance affect his mental state? Instead of falling back on the tried-and-true descriptions of hair color, eye color, and one or two dominant personality traits, consider what truly defines each of your characters. What makes them unique individuals, different from all others? Choose the information—whether it comes in the form of physical appearance, body language, or backstory—that will best reveal your character to your reader, and you'll find that your story will come to life.

Teen Character Choices

- **Age:** There's a huge difference between twelve and eighteen. How old do you want your character to be? What kind of issues will your book address? Who is your target audience?

- **Physical appearance:** Physical appearance can be even more important to teens than it is to adults. What does your character look like, and how does she feel about her appearance? How does her appearance shape her body language?

- **Life experience:** What factors shape your character's choices? Has your teen lived a sheltered life or a worldly one? What does he know about sex? Has he ever tried drugs or alcohol? Has he traveled on his own? What events in his past have had the most influence on his personality?

Family relationships: Since teens live at home, parents and siblings are an important factor in their daily existence. How does your teen character interact with her family? How does she treat her siblings? Does she antagonize her parents? Use her actions to reveal the family dynamics.

The clique factor: Friends are so important to teens! Who is your character's best friend? How does your teen fit into the social categories that exist in his environment? Is he popular? Picked on? Ignored? How does he treat others?

Aspirations: Teens are often looking toward the future. What does your character want to do after high school or college? What kind of person does she hope to become? Is she optimistic or pessimistic about the future of this planet?

PASSIVE VS. ACTIVE CHARACTERS

Have you ever heard an editor or a critic refer to a character as passive? Maybe, like me, you've found yourself frustrated by this term. What exactly does it mean, and what's so bad about creating a passive character? Isn't this a trait we often find in real people, especially certain teenagers, who can be prone to spending long hours watching TV or playing videogames?

Since passive people do exist in life, it took me a long time to understand why a passive character so seldom works in the context of a novel. It wasn't until I tried unsuccessfully to write a novel featuring a passive character that I learned what makes this trait so difficult to portray. Hopefully, this section will save you lots of misspent time and effort.

If you're considering writing about a passive character, or if you're told by others that your existing characters seem too passive, consider this: Passive people might be described as submissive or failing to take initiative. They are acted upon more than they act. When you look at this description side by side with the statement above about characters being revealed by what they do and say, the picture should begin to come into focus. How do we know who a character is if he doesn't act? How will you breathe life into him if he doesn't make any choices?

While it's true that we all know people in real life who seem to drift along on the tide, never taking much initiative to affect their circumstances, we don't necessarily want to read about them. We're all familiar with the stereotype of the antisocial teen who hides out in her bedroom, but would you want to read a book about that person? Not only is it hard for the audience to figure out who she is, it's tough to invest in her journey because there's nothing she's looking to learn or accomplish.

Active characters, on the other hand, are endlessly fascinating because we're always wondering what they'll do next. It's easy to feel as if we know them well, and when a reader feels like they know a character in the same way they know a real person, they'll invest in loving him, hating him, rooting for him, or laughing with him. Active characters shape the plot through the choices they make, and their desires create mirrored desires in the audience.

As a writer, you have two very powerful tools for creating active characters: actions and dialogue. Active characters use plenty of both. They make choices, doing and saying things that lead to new choices and new actions, advancing the plot. Use these tools to your advantage. Give your characters plenty to say and do. Make them leap, make them dance, make them cry, and make them laugh. In short, make them live. You'll keep both your characters *and* your audience engaged in your story.

USING ACTION TO DEFINE CHARACTER

Contrary to what many people think, action isn't just about plot. Actions also reveal character. What a person does shows us who he is—not just who he says he is. We all know how this works in real life. How many of us had a classmate who was saccharine sweet on the outside but talked with an acid tongue as soon as someone else's back was turned? Do you remember the shy girl who never said a word, but when courage was needed she was the first one who stepped up? Or how about the popular guy who acted conceited until he was alone, then he couldn't stop talking about his little brothers and sisters?

When we watch a person make choices, we're able to gauge many things about her. How passionately does she truly feel about something? Is she capable of sacrifice? Cowardice? Love? Maybe she's more afraid then she's letting on.

The revelatory power of our actions is no less true in fiction. In fact, it's probably even more necessary on the page, where a story exists for only one reader at a time and there's no one to ask for a second opinion. The best example of this power is the use of the unreliable narrator. When an author uses this technique, the character is telling the audience one thing, but the audience is expected to come to a different conclusion based on the character's actions.

How can this be accomplished? We do it by showing what a character *does*, not just what he says.

In my book *Saint Iggy*, I used the unreliable narrator technique to create a portrait of a young man who is having a hard time figuring out his true nature. In the beginning of the book Iggy has just been kicked out of school, and he relates the story from a point of view that is distinctly his own, minimizing his role in causing the trouble and placing much of the blame squarely on others. However, the reader, being outside the situation, sees Iggy's actions in addition to his words and can question his version of events.

Here's the account of his expulsion as related by Iggy in play format:

> Me: (coming in late to Spanish class because I followed a hot new girl) Can I sit here?
>
> Mrs. Brando: (confused) I think you have the wrong classroom.
>
> Me: (correctly) No, I'm in this class.
>
> Mrs. Brando: (really patronizing) Son, it is December and I have not seen you in this class even once before, so I don't know what classroom you are looking for. Are you new here, too?
>
> Me: (being real patient) Nooo, I am in this class and if you'd just check your list from the beginning of the year you'd see that. (under my breath really freaking quietly) Bitch.
>
> Mrs. Brando: (spazzing out) Are you threatening me? Do you have a weapon? Are you on drugs? Someone get the principal. Call security. Help! Help! Help!

Even as Iggy tells his story, which is obviously highly dramatized, his actions give us a different sense of things. He's come in late to a class he doesn't really belong in and he calls the teacher a bitch. Although he's trying to tell us that the teacher was being unreasonable and patronizing, the audience doesn't quite buy it. Throughout the novel, Iggy oscillates between low self-esteem and grandiose ideas of what he can accomplish, and it's up to the reader to decide, based on the choices he makes, whether Iggy is ultimately a saint or a villain.

If you are using the unreliable narrator technique, make sure your character's actions are not interpreted for the reader by the narrator. The most important element in creating this kind of character is trusting your reader to reach her own conclusions. Let your character's actions become the palette through which you, as the author, influence your audience.

When your characters take action, their actions can speak louder than your words. In *Saint Iggy*, I deliberately made Iggy's actions ambiguous so the reader would have to question her definition of his character, but it's possible to make a character's motives quite clear as well. Want your tough guy to be a saint? Or your perfect student to be a villain? Show the reader what the character *does* and he will see your character's true nature. Remember that a reader brings with him all of his own life experiences and most of us, by the time we reach our teenage years, have developed a good sense of human nature. We're capable of seeing what people do and, based on that, discerning a piece of who they are. No matter what, don't be afraid to let your reader use his judgment.

DIALOGUE

Dialogue is another important tool for defining character. Teenagers don't act in a vacuum. They talk about their lives with their friends, family, teachers, and significant others. In fact, according to many parents, they talk, and talk, and talk. Just look at the average teen's cell phone bill! These conversations both shape and reveal who a person is. Like action, dialogue is a way for a character's true personality to show without you, as the author, having to explicitly state the message you're trying to get across. And unlike a deliberately stated explanation, dialogue draws a reader in.

Imagine a teacher standing at the front of a packed classroom lecturing. After a while, the students start shifting in their seats and sneaking glances at their watches. Straight exposition can only hold our attention for so long. In a teen novel, that time period is mercilessly short.

Dialogue, however, works in an entirely different manner. Imagine that same teacher standing in the hallway whispering to another teacher. Now they truly have your attention and they can hold it for a lot longer because of the "What ifs" created by the format. In dialogue we are constantly wondering what someone will say and how the other person will respond. Dialogue is unpredictable, which makes it fascinating.

From a technical writing standpoint, dialogue also creates white space, which breaks up big blocks of exposition that might otherwise be tiresome and monotonous. Virginia Euwer Wolff said this about white space during an interview with *The Horn Book*:

> I myself am intimidated by huge pages of gray without any white space. I wanted the white space to thread through the story and give it room to breathe. That sounds a little pretentious but it's kind of what I meant to do. I wanted the friendliness of white space on a page.

Dialogue is a great way to create space, inviting readers in and keeping the pace of your book sharp and quick. Let's look at how E.R. Frank uses dialogue in her novel *America* to draw you into the story. Here are a few lines from the beginning of the book between a character in a mental hospital and a nurse.

> "Step off," I tell this nurse when she tries to get me
> to eat.
>   "You mean, thank you for caring," she says. "You're
> welcome."
>   "I need a lighter," I tell her, and she goes, "You mean
> you want a lighter. Dream on, sweetheart."

How the characters speak to each other gives us great insight into who they are. In just a few lines, we're able to see the main character as resentful and rebellious, and we understand the nurse to be caring yet firm, with a wry sense of humor. No one tells us this directly, but we're able to intuit it through what the characters say. At the same time, what they don't say invites us to ask questions about what's going on and what's brought each character to this place.

By using dialogue, you can create an intimate tone, letting your audience feel as if they're overhearing something interesting, even while the main character withholds information that isn't revealed until the end of the book. Remember to use both the positive (what is said) and the negative (what isn't said) as you craft your conversations on the page. Read them aloud to make sure they sound natural, and inspect your pages to make sure there's plenty of white space in your manuscript. If you notice long, solid blocks of black print, chances are you don't have enough dialogue. Go back and give your characters a chance to speak!

BODY LANGUAGE

Body language is a combination of action and dialogue, and it can be a very powerful tool. When done well, body language can add a subtle layer underneath the overt action, enhancing what your characters are saying and doing, and giving your audience additional insight into the scene you're creating.

We all read each other's body language in real life, so why not let it work for you in your fiction? That scowl you've seen flitting across your mother-in-law's face? Bring it to life on the face of your character's boss at the mall. The tension that creeps into your friend's shoulders every time she talks about her past? Study the way she reacts and use it to paint a picture for your readers that hints at something your character isn't revealing. Don't be afraid to let your characters itch, twitch, squirm, and squint.

Here's how body language worked for me in this scene from *Fat Kid Rules the World*. In this passage the main character, three hundred-pound Troy Billings, is observing the reactions around him as his semi-homeless, usually hyper friend Curt, joins his ex-marine father and sports fanatic little brother for dinner. Watch how body language sets the stage, cementing the character dynamics before the conversation even begins.

> I sit next to the roast beef and mashed potatoes, and Dad passes the peas and bread. As usual, Dayle hogs the quart of milk. We wait for Curt to sit down, but he stands in the doorway looking nervous before sliding in next to Dayle. He folds his hands as if he's about to pray, looks up, notices we're not praying, and unfolds them guiltily. Dad glances at the clock to indicate that

we've lingered too long, but he doesn't say anything. Just passes the bread to Curt.

There's a lot of shuffling as the food gets passed and I sit back to watch the drama. It's twisted of me, I know, but I kind of enjoy the intense discomfort of it all. Everyone looks pained and for once I'm not the cause. Tonight, I am the most comfortable person in the room. I watch them all like a sociologist.

First, there's Curt. I know Curt's uncomfortable because he's restrained. He doesn't show any excitement except in the corners of his eyes and he's very careful to sit still. His napkin falls off his lap repeatedly, and every time it does, he glares at it as if it's betrayed him. When he bends down to pick it up, he tries not to bend his body, as if that might count as too much movement. Soon he's engaged in an all-out secret battle with the napkin that culminates in a covert stabbing with his fork.

Then there's Dad. I know Dad's uncomfortable because he doesn't speak. He limits himself to nods of encouragement or censure and keeps his posture perfect. This means he has to stifle his desire to correct Curt's posture, which is not perfect. Consequently, his grip on his knife tightens until his fingers turn completely white.

And of course, there's Dayle. I know Dayle's uncomfortable because ... well, I wouldn't have known it if I hadn't seen him dish the roast beef, but as soon as he lifts the serving fork I know. He takes

Writing & Selling the *ya novel*

one portion instead of five even though he's desperate to gain weight, and he never once looks at Curt as he passes the tray.

Curt, however, takes five helpings, then puts half of it back. Then he retakes half of the half he just put back.

Dad takes a deep breath as the scene repeats itself with the mashed potatoes. And the peas. And the bread. Finally, Dad can't stand it any longer. He sets down his knife and turns to Curt.

"So," he says. "Do you have a job?"

See how the characters' mannerisms help us understand who they are and what they're feeling? Without having read any other part of this book, do you already have a sense of the personalities involved?

Body language is a wonderful tool for rounding out a scene, making it both real and complex. Use it wisely and use it well. You'll soon find that your scenes take on a multidimensional quality they might have been lacking before.

WORDS OF CAUTION

Body language and dialogue are two of the best ways to bring characters to life, but I would offer a few words of caution, especially regarding dialogue. Characters in books do not speak the same way people in real life speak. Most of us ramble, cutting off sentences in the middle and never getting back to them. We allow our train of thought to take us off the topic of conversation. Some of us might repeat the same actions, like twitching or blinking or scratching, far more than we're aware. We say "um," "like," and "you know" so often that we cease to hear them.

If you've ever had to take dictation you understand what I mean. When you read through an actual transcript of a conversation it's nearly impossible to follow. While writers strive for realism, this is not something we want to emulate. Remember that dialogue is meant to reveal character, not writing prowess. The goal for any given scene is not to convince a reader you are the most talented mimic of all time. In fact, it's quite the opposite. In the best scenes the writer fades into the background so much so that the reader forgets the writer exists. The reader has suspended his disbelief to the point where he feels as if he is listening to a conversation between two real people. For this to happen, he can't be stumbling over words and sentences laden with "likes" and "ums" and he can't be fighting a nagging sense that no one really talks in such a polished, grammatically correct manner. You, as the author, must strike a balance.

Dialogue, as well as first-person narrative (the "I" voice), is all about weighing what sounds real against what makes for clean reading. A good rule of thumb is that a little goes a long way. Do you feel your teen character would say "like" a lot? Well, one strategically placed "like" can have more impact than the more realistic dozens of uses because the flow of the text is not interrupted. The same can be applied to accents and regional words. Certainly people from different parts of the world speak differently, using unique slang and speech patterns, but trying to force too many examples of this into your writing can backfire, taking away from the intended effect. Dialogue is a powerful tool, but choose your characters' words wisely. Remember, writing is not about capturing speech verbatim—it's about using rhythm and word choice to capture the truth of what your characters say. How the words translate to the reader is more important than how they would sound in real life. To facilitate this, many authors read their dialogue out loud. You might need to write several versions of a conversation before you reach that critical balance that makes your characters seem real while not interrupting the reading experience.

cautious at the same time. He could be your best friend or your worst enemy.

Kirstin, age 16, Michigan: Edward from *Twilight* by Stephenie Meyer. I fell in love with him on the first page.

Rebecca, age 16, New Mexico: A character that I will remember forever is Holden Caulfield from *The Catcher in the Rye*. What made me fall in love with this character was my ability to relate to him. I found him interesting because he seemed more than capable to surpass any task he faced with ease but did as he pleased instead of doing what was asked of him.

TYPES OF CHARACTERS

Once you understand action and dialogue as tools for developing characters, the question arises: Who do you give the actions and dialogue *to*? When you have many different characters, how can you decide which character gets to speak that great line or make that important decision?

When you begin a story, it's important to be very clear about whose story you're telling. When I critique manuscripts, one of the most common problems I find is confusion over who the main character is. Sometimes a character that seems to be set up in the beginning of the novel as the primary character ends up with the least amount of action and dialogue. Thus the character arc lacks fulfillment. Instead of feeling most attached to that character, I lose interest in his struggle.

This is an easy trap to fall into. Many writers relate experiences where characters they intended to keep in the background gain prominence as the story progresses. Characters can take on lives of their own, which is great because it allows for spontaneity as we create our novels, but when push comes to shove, it's still our job to make sure the right story gets told. Sometimes, that story might truly belong to a character other than the one we thought was the main character. If so, this will involve going back to square one to start over again. But more often than not, what needs to happen is for you to be clear in your own mind about who the main character is and what that character's story arc should be.

Remember this: The main character is the one the story is about. She is the one whose actions should most affect the plot. Can there be more than one main character? Yes, in certain circumstances such as novels told in alternating chapters, this can work, but generally it's difficult for the audience to be truly invested in more than one set of goals. This is not to say there won't be other major characters with story arcs of their own. A secondary character can even end up being a reader's *favorite* character, but in the end, the story is not his, and if it was, it would be told very differently.

Secondary characters exist to interact with the main character. They might be fabulous, interesting, hilarious, or brilliant, but if they didn't relate to the main character's story, we wouldn't know about them. Consider comic books as an example. Every hero has a sidekick, and while he is central to the story, he never takes over the main character's role.

In addition to the main character and major secondary characters, there are also minor characters who play smaller roles in your main character's life. I've often heard these characters likened to extras on a movie set. Some extras have speaking roles and they might reappear during the course of the movie, but others will only be seen in the background, never being named or clearly defined. In fact, whether you give a character a name is an important clue to your readers as to the level of that character's importance.

With every character you create, be sure the amount of time you spend developing them is proportional to their importance. Let your reader know right from the start who your main character is and be consistent throughout. The most action and dialogue should go to your main character and the major secondary characters she interacts with.

STEREOTYPES

So, if your main character is supposed to be the one you develop the most, how can you bring minor characters to life? This is a tricky issue, but there are times when stereotypes can be used to a writer's advantage. In our society we do our best to avoid conventional forms, but a writer must be aware of readers' prefabricated notions and either use them as a quick way to shed light on background characters or destroy them as necessary.

When dealing with your main character and your major secondary characters, stereotypes should either be avoided or given a surprise twist so your reader doesn't feel like he is reading a cliché. When a major character relies too heavily on stereotypes, your reader will feel like he's read your story before and it will be difficult for him to suspend his disbelief. However, if you take a conventional character type, such as the popular cheerleader, and give her companion traits the reader isn't expecting—a MENSA IQ perhaps, or maybe a rebellious streak and a penchant for tattoos—this will wake the reader up again. We're interested in what's unfamiliar. That's why characters with interesting quirks are so attractive.

Think back to your first period history assignment. It might be helpful to recall how many books have come before yours and how many different characters readers have already seen and interacted with. You want your characters to be one of a kind, not only so you're not copying what might already have been done, but also because unique characters will make unique choices that will drive the plot in directions no one expects. Including you!

The times you can use stereotypes without subverting them are when you're developing minor background characters you want your reader to be able to recognize without taking the time to tell that character's entire story, or when you're using parody or humor and want to poke fun at the stereotype itself.

Orson Scott Card says in his book *Characters & Viewpoint*:

> If we think that a particular stereotype is unfair to a group it supposedly explains, then we're free to deliberately violate the stereotype. But the moment we do that, we have made the character strange, which will make him attract the readers' attention. He will no longer simply disappear—he isn't a walk-on anymore. He has stepped forward out of the milieu and joined the story.

Stereotypes can be a tool, allowing the reader to feel like he knows a minor, insignificant character, or they can be a launching pad for creating an against-type character, but either way they must be used judiciously. When you choose to use a stereotype, you not only risk boring your readers, you risk offending them. Choose your risks wisely.

YOUR MOST VALUABLE PLAYERS

No matter what type of characters you decide to create, remember that, when done well, characterization can be your most valuable tool. It's the characters your readers must root for, sympathize with, or despise, and the more real your characters seem, the more real the story will become to your audience.

Take time to study the teens you interact with in your daily life. See if they have traits you can use. Human beings are complex, and this complexity makes us endlessly fascinating. Characters you vividly portray, exploring their nuances and delving into their motivations, contradictions, and emotions, will draw your teen readers in and allow them to gain insight into themselves as they recognize pieces of who they are in what your characters do and say.

Our teenage years are characterized by exploration of the world as we transition from childhood to adulthood. Experiences are new and intense, and our passage to self-discovery is at a critical juncture. As teens recognize the places of darkness and light within the characters we create, they will also begin to recognize those places within themselves. We owe it to them to dig deeply, offering more than what is on the surface of human nature.

As an author for young adults, you have the opportunity to bring to life characters that will stick with your readers long after they have closed your book, illuminating aspects of human nature that might otherwise have remained in the dark. You have the chance to influence your readers at a time when they are still forming their worldviews and discovering themselves. This is both the solemn responsibility and the great joy of writing YA novels.

Homework: Take one of your ideas from 2nd period and develop several different characters who could act as your main character. Try subverting stereotypes to work to your advantage. For example, if your plot involved a student with a crush on a young male teacher, you could make that student:

- a punk girl who is rebellious but effortlessly gets good grades

- a young man who excels in drama but wishes he could make the football team

- a deaf student who has trouble making herself understood

Look at the ways each character would affect the plot. Even the identity of the teacher might be dependent on how you draw your main character. For example, the punk girl's teacher might be an AP History teacher who is attractive to the girl because he allows her to connect to the world instead of shunning it. For the young man who yearns to be on the football team, the teacher might also be the football coach. Pay special attention to which characters seem most interesting to you. Which ones do you feel you could most easily develop? What draws you to them?

4th PERIOD

LUNCH

A Plateful of Heathly Plot

If there's one thing that remains vivid from my teen years it's the school lunchroom. I can still recall the smell—it was never a clear smell, always an amalgam. For me, there was a feeling of nausea that was both related and unrelated to that scent. The odd thing is, I spent very little time in the lunchroom because most days I wiled away my lunch period in the choir rehearsal rooms. So why does the lunch experience stand out so vividly?

I can answer that in one word: drama. There was always something happening in the cafeteria and most of the time it wasn't good. The lunchroom meant making difficult choices—forming alliances as you chose where to sit and figuring out how to avoid the more obvious pitfalls of unwittingly stepping into someone else's territory or, heaven forbid, tripping while carrying your lunch tray. There were consequences to these actions. One wrong move and you might be the object of the nearest bully's ridicule or the laughingstock of the whole school. Entire reputations could be made or shattered in the lunchroom.

This is what plot is all about. Good plots have something at stake. They're full of the triumphs and heartbreaks that make us human, and there are consequences to every decision. They take navigating, and it isn't easy to wind your way through.

To explore the essentials of plot, it's necessary to look closely at conflict, believability, and resolution. These three things make up the engine that will drive your book forward, taking readers along for the ride before depositing them safely home again. Once you understand the heart of plot, it's possible to look into the mechanics of developing a story line from start to finish.

WHY CONFLICT?

Conflict isn't fun. In real life, most of us avoid it like the plague. It's ironic, then, that nothing can draw us into a book faster than a good dose of conflict. Take a look at these first sentences from popular YA novels:

> They promised me nine years of safety but only gave me three. (*Such a Pretty Girl* by Laura Wiess)

> "Dear Lord," prayed Mercy Carter, "do not let us be murdered in our beds tonight." (*The Ransom of Mercy Carter* by Caroline B. Cooney)

> Things had been getting a little better until I got a letter from my dead sister. (*Dead Girls Don't Write Letters* by Gail Giles)

What do they all have in common? They open with conflict. It's clear right from the start that all is not well, and instantly the reader wants to know more. How did the situation get to this point? How will it be resolved?

Our interest in conflict is threefold. First, and most importantly, it provides that page-turning quality where we can't wait to know what happens next. Without conflict, a reader can pretty much guess what will happen in the story because no one will do anything surprising or tantalizing or outside the bounds of the familiar. With conflict, the options are abundant, and the only way to find out what really happens is to turn the page.

Second, conflict inspires strong emotions, both in your characters and your readers. When we're drawn into the tension an author has created, we allow ourselves to live vicariously through the book. Although we might not want to feel terror or grief or anger in our own life, experiencing it through the filter of a character's life gives us a chance to explore that emotion without consequences to ourselves.

Third, as we learned in English class, conflict can be a way to explore character development because how a person handles a given situation tells us a lot about him. Most people are naturally curious about our fellow human beings and when we read, we see people in action—people faced with tough decisions—so we have a chance to observe and judge their choices.Conflict is present in every genre. It's even present in books we might perceive as "light" reading. That teen romance novel your fifteen-year-old niece packs for the beach? It's full of conflict. If the guy and girl started out together there would be no need to keep reading. That humorous new Louise Rennison novel that will make you laugh until you cry? There's plenty of conflict. Just read *Angus, Thongs and Full-Frontal Snogging* and you'll see that main character Georgia Nicolson's life is no walk in the park. How could she make us laugh so much if she didn't get into precarious situations that constantly required outlandish solutions?

There are many different types of conflict that can affect our characters. Sometimes that conflict is delicious, like sexual tension crackling between two characters who haven't yet admitted their love, and other times it's dangerous, like the cloak-and-dagger events surrounding a teenage spy. Sometimes conflict takes the form of grief or embarrassment or pain. But always, it's the anticipation of resolution that keeps us turning the pages to learn the outcome.

BELIEVABILITY

As we turn the pages, there's one important quality that can't be ignored: believability. If plots are driven by the conflict that is set up in the beginning of the book, believability is a reader's willingness to suspend his disbelief and go along with the story as it unfolds. This is not to be confused with realism. Realism means representing things as they are in reality, but believability has little to do with reality and everything to do with your reader's state of mind.

Have you ever had the experience of being so immersed in a fantasy novel that you forget the characters aren't human? Have you jumped when reading a horror novel? Cried when reading a love story even though the events portrayed are clearly outside the realm of anything that would ever happen in real life? That's believability.

You want your readers to be so immersed in your characters and story that they forget they are reading a book. This is a particular challenge when writing for teens because teens are so aware of different forms of media. They are inundated with stories on TV and in movie theaters, and these days, with the prevalence of behind-the-scenes shows and DVD bonus features, they know a lot more about the mechanics of how stories are put together and marketed than they used to. If a story seems contrived, a teen will be instantly catapulted out of the book. Instead of caring what happens, she'll be thinking, "This isn't real."

Believability is important, so when you're crafting your plot, make sure you choose characters and events that draw a reader in, inviting her to suspend her disbelief. Much of this quality will come from your writing style, but some of it will come from the choices you make and the choices your characters make. If you're writing realistic fiction, be aware not only of what *is* true, but of what your readers will perceive as true. Both are important.

Maintaining Believability for Teens

- **Don't let your authorial voice intrude.** Avoid adding your own personal commentary to your plot. Let your characters react instead.

- **Don't strain your credibility.** It might be believable that a character could survive a high-speed car crash, but don't let her emerge miraculously unscathed. Stay within the bounds of expectation.

- **Avoid stereotypes and clichés.** When a reader has seen or heard something before, it causes him to think about the fact that he's reading a story. He won't be able to immerse himself in the experience of reading your book. Keep your characters and plot lines as varied and unique as real life.

- **Make sure your plot isn't stretched too far.** Even the most willing reader will become skeptical if events keep unfolding long beyond the point where they should have been resolved. Know when to wrap things up.

- **Use realistic dialogue.** Nothing screams fake like using language that teens wouldn't use. It isn't about what you would say, but what your readers and characters would say!

- **Be consistent.** Whatever the rules of your world are, stay within them. Don't change anything for your own convenience.

RESOLUTION

No matter what type of conflict you set up at the beginning of your novel, it must have some kind of resolution by the end. This is a basic tenet of plot, and at first glance it might seem flat-out wrong—what about the countless novels that leave us hanging, suspended without knowing the fate of the main character? What about books where the hero dies or the couple doesn't end up together? Certainly we can all think of books that don't wrap things up neatly at the end.

But resolution in writing has little to do with wrapping everything up. In fact, unless you're writing a deliberately formulaic novel, the more perfectly you tie everything up, the more likely a reader is to find your story hard to believe. Readers recognize that stories reflect life— even if that life takes place on another planet or in a fantasy world of our own creation—so they expect at least some degree of ambiguity.

Writing & Selling the *ya novel*

Resolution in novels has more to do with carrying a theme from beginning to end than with providing an answer to a stated problem. I've heard it said that when a reader begins a book, she makes an unspoken contract with the author. That contract is shaped by the type of book she's picked up (the genre, the design, the promotion, etc.) and by the setup the author imposes in the beginning of the novel. If an author starts out writing a thriller, the audience wants it to remain a thriller until the end. If the main character begins by making a plan to find his long-lost father, we want to see whether he accomplishes his goal. Even if he does *not* accomplish his goal, we want to hear how the quest has changed him along the way.

Many, many times resolutions are not satisfying in the sense of making us happy or erasing all questions from our minds. They can be infuriating or painful. They can leave you hanging, asking yourself more questions than when you began. But there must always be some acknowledgment of where you began when you end. Not a literal stated acknowledgment, but a sense of a journey taken and fulfilled.

Plots have beginnings, middles, and ends, and endings are what you leave your readers with, so it's important to ask yourself how you want to affect them. Even if you want to leave your readers yearning for more, you still need to give them some sense of completion.

Try mapping out your novel on paper. Write down each of your main characters and chart the journey that character makes. Does each character arc have a beginning, middle, and end? Does each character change in some way? Do they accomplish the purpose you set for them? Or did you leave them hanging?

Do the same thing for each theme or conflict you introduce. Which themes are present from the beginning to the end of your novel? Are any of them abandoned midway through? Which conflicts are resolved and which ones are left unresolved? Were your choices realistic?

Resolution is an important part of any plot. The ending of your book is the last thing a reader will think about before he's done reading. Spending the extra time to make sure you've gotten everything right will allow your book to be remembered for all the right reasons instead of all the wrong ones.

Teen Panel

DO YOU FIND TEEN NOVELS SET IN THE MODERN DAY TO BE TRUE TO LIFE? WHAT DO BOOKS GET RIGHT ABOUT BEING A TEEN TODAY? WHAT DO THEY GET WRONG?

Alexis, age 13, Pennsylvania: Most of the books I've read have gotten the average teen's life right. We do go through a lot at school. We do go through hard decisions. Being a teen isn't as easy as it looks. In some books the teen's whole life depends on who they're dating or who they like. For me, it's not like that at all.

Long, age 17, California: Modern day "teen novels" tend to be acceptable for the most part. The same old, same old situations and problems that every teen goes through can get redundant if not predictable. What novels need to be today, in short, is *smarter*. Teens are much more attentive and intelligent in this age of information, and the movie industry and television have introduced us to complex plot sequences and challenging presentation. Novels should be more challenging and engaging or, if anything, more

Writing & Selling the *YA novel*

experimental; something both the writer and reader must devote time to for the real rewards to make themselves evident.

Erin, age 16, Idaho: Emotion is key to writing believable teen characters because we go through so many. Whether it's emotions concerning body image, peer pressure, wanting a dream more than anything, friendship problems, multiple heartaches—our lives are full of *emotions*. Thus, emotion-ridden characters ring most true. The teen books I've read don't get a lot wrong—especially since there are so many different teens out there with different perspectives. There are always new areas to explore.

Shelby, age 15, New Mexico: Yes and no. Mostly they get the hardships right, but the formation of relationships happen too fast.

Marissa, age 12, New York: Of the novels that I've read, they are true to life. Some of the novels talk about fear, guilt and depression. Sometimes an author doesn't talk about death the way people really feel about it.

Sydney, age 17, Michigan: Some of them are true to life, yes. A lot of the time I find the characters fall in love too easily. Conversations go too well. It's all very programmed. Authors tend to get the internal thoughts right though.

Sierra, age 15, New York: I find teen novels to be true to some extent. What they get right is the sense of loneliness, uncertainty, peer pressure, and wanting to be liked. What they get wrong sometimes is the over dramatization of characters. Sometimes I think to myself, "Would someone I know really say that?"

STRUCTURE AND DECISION MAKING

Now that you know the basics on which a plot hinges, it's time to get down to the nuts and bolts. When you're sitting in front of a blank computer screen, how do you begin to organize events so there's plenty of conflict, a satisfying resolution, and enough credibility for your readers? You've got the idea and you've got the characters, but you need the structure.

How will you tell the story? Will you tell it in a linear fashion where events unfold as they would in real life? Maybe you'll want to use flashbacks. Should you reveal everything from the start or should you hide key pieces of information to be parceled out as the story moves along? Could you open from the point of view of the bad guy and then switch to that of the good guy later on or should your point of view remain consistent?

Each of these decisions is dependent on the type of story you're telling and your strengths as a writer. Young adult is a broad category, and different genres within the boundary of YA fiction have different styles of writing associated with them. You'll want to be aware of what those styles are in case you want to use them. For example, it's common for fantasy novels to open with a scene featuring the villain. Mysteries are usually dependent on the author keeping certain information hidden from the reader. Romance is commonly written from multiple points of view.

But for every rule there are exceptions, and being aware of how other authors have organized their plots does not mean you have to make the same choices. Instead, assume that common formats are used precisely because they work well for that style of book, but balance this against how *you* want to tell the story and what you know your strengths and weaknesses to be. Maybe you can never get flashbacks right or crawling into the head of a villain always ends up sounding false when you attempt it. Deciding how to organize your plot should come from the story itself and shouldn't be forced.

Ask yourself the following questions to help you decide what form your plot should take:

- Who is telling the story and what are her motives?
- What kind of mood would you like to create?
- How fast should the pace of the book be?
- Is any aspect of the story dependent on a need for secrecy?
- How important is your antagonist?
- How much time passes from beginning to end?
- Do you need to accommodate multiple points of view?

As you answer these questions, you can begin to determine what format is right for your story. Linear forms lend themselves to fast pacing. Flashbacks slow down the action, allowing the reader to take a breather. They can easily be used to create a nostalgic or sentimental tone. Alternating chapters can allow you to look at the same event multiple times. A combination of these techniques might allow you to accommodate many points of view and piece out information slowly to your reader. Just beware of using forms simply for the sake of the form. The simplest way of telling the story is almost always the best. Remember that any writing technique risks calling attention to itself, pulling your reader out of the story, so keep believability in mind.

ORGANIZING YOUR PLOTS AND SUBPLOTS

Once you've made some basic decisions about the form your plot will take, it's time to start planning things out—what will happen when.

Writers approach this task in many different ways. Some writers use outlines. This allows them to think out each plot element ahead of time and saves a lot of confusion and rewriting along the way.

Other writers use various systems of note taking, or more loosely based methods of gathering ideas. If you write your notes on index cards, for example, those cards can be shuffled again and again to try out different time lines. If you're still unsure about what form you want your plot to take, this can be an excellent way to experiment without actually writing the text. This approach is similar to the storyboards that moviemakers use.

Some authors know only the basics of their story when they set out and have to discover the plot of their book along the way. I've always been this type of writer. I usually have one or two key scenes in mind, but other than that I let the characters direct the story. This can be a tricky approach because you can easily write yourself into a corner or stray too far from the path of your plot. But when it works, it allows for the most freedom and surprises.

No matter which approach you choose (or perhaps you'll come up with one of your own) the important thing to remember when creating your plot is to make sure there is something that ties everything together from beginning to end. I like to imagine a straight line running through my books. That line is my theme, or my central dilemma, and no matter what happens around it, the line must be present.

But what about subplots? How do they fit in? What if there's more than one theme? Plots and subplots are similar to main characters and secondary characters. There's almost always one main character, and although you can develop several major secondary characters, if you try to develop too many the book becomes crowded and the reader starts wondering, "Whose story is this anyway?"

Just as the secondary characters exist to help tell the main character's tale, subplots work to strengthen and enhance the main plot. A love story subplot can release tension through humor or sentiment, or it can create tension if the love interest ends up in danger. Either way it can enhance the experience of the characters in the book. A parent's developmental subplot in a teen drama might round out the depiction of the character's world, or it could juxtapose the decisions the main character makes with the decisions of his parent. Subplots are wonderful ways to enrich your novel so long as they exist to further the main story line.

A metaphor I find helpful when balancing plots and subplots is the image of weaving a tapestry. When I start a novel, I imagine each plot and subplot as a strand of colored thread. I have all those strands in my hands as I begin, and I must have all of them in my hands as I end. The colors will overlap and intertwine, but there's one dominant shape or picture they're all working to create. The important thing is not to let any threads go and to make sure each stays in its rightful place.

What kind of tapestry are you creating? Whether you know exactly what it will look like beforehand or you want to be surprised, you've got to have a recognizable pattern by the end. Weave your threads carefully so your end result will be an artistic creation and not a mess of threads.

PACING AND SUBSTANCE FOR YOUNG ADULTS

No discussion of plots in a book about writing for young adults would be complete without addressing the questions of pacing and substance for teenagers. The authors of books for teens must ask themselves not only how to create, organize, and balance their plots and subplots, but also how teen readers will respond to the events unfolding in the story.

You might wonder why I didn't begin the chapter with this section. Why not set our boundaries right from the start so we don't waste time? If there are content or forms that are off-limits, shouldn't we know that before we begin? These are good questions, but they also have a good answer.

Writing for teens is not about limits, it's about possibilities.

Deciding to be a YA author is not about confining yourself within the limitations of established rules; it's about writing with the maximum integrity for an audience that is intelligent, complex, and primed to explore.

We'll talk more about hot-button issues like language, sex, and violence at the end of this book, but for the purposes of creating the plot of your novel, know that YA literature is full of diverse examples of almost every form imaginable. YA plots range from fast-paced, first-person narratives to meandering trips back and forth in time, and they cover everything in between.

That said, you should be aware that most YA books are shorter than their adult counterparts, so unless your book is an exception to the rule, your pacing will need to vary accordingly. In teen literature every word must count, and there isn't always room for long passages of description or exposition. Instead of stretching a plot for 400 pages, you will most likely be fitting it into about 250 pages.

The same is true for content issues. Although almost any subject can be written about for teenagers these days, you still want to write a book that is appealing and relevant to your audience. Remember that the one defining characteristic of YA literature is its audience, so you want each facet of your plot—from beginning to middle to end—to reflect, entertain, or challenge today's teens. Ultimately, it's what you believe teens are capable of reading and enjoying that will define your choices about what will happen in your novel.

Homework:

Look at the following books for teens:

Monster
by Walter Dean Myers

A Northern Light
by Jennifer Donnelly

Keesha's House
by Helen Frost

Sloppy Firsts by Megan McCafferty

Art Attack by Marc Aronson

ttfn by Lauren Myracle

The Perks of Being a Wallflower by Stephen Chboksy

Notice all the different ways that the authors have organized their plots. These books represent various formats such as scripts, diaries, poetry, and multimedia. They're told from the present, past, and future. Read the jacket copy to get a sense of the plot. Then read the first few pages of each book. Do you get an immediate sense of conflict? What kind of pace has the author set? Where do you think the story will go?

5th PERIOD

SOCIAL STUDIES

Studying Settings From Every Time and Place

How many of you took Social Studies in school? Remember the way the world map was usually on a roller and the teacher would pull it down like a window shade? Remember those thick, battered textbooks, packed with information we took for granted was true? Now we might look back on those same textbooks and cringe at their interpretation of events. Christopher Columbus, who once "discovered" America, now "colonized" it. The "radical" idea of desegregation is now something we can't believe was any other way. Our understanding of the world has changed over time just as the world around us has evolved into what it is today.

For writers, understanding our characters' world and their place in it is part and parcel of understanding the real world we live in. As our characters are influenced by and interact with the settings we create for them, we have a chance to explore different places around the globe, different time periods, and different cultures. When

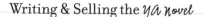

writing for teens, we may be introducing our readers to these places for the first time, so it's important our settings be as true as we can make them. The exceptions, of course, will be genres like fantasy, science fiction, or horror, where settings can be highly stylized rather than realistic. But even in these cases, you'll want to choose the very best descriptions so your setting *seems* real and has the most impact possible.

When done well, settings can shape our stories and create a tone that helps an author achieve his or her goals. The easiest way to understand this is to imagine a photograph of a person. Without the background, that person could be anyone, anywhere, but with it, the details of the moment become much clearer. Seeing a person within a setting helps us understand him. It creates an image of who he is and what he's doing.

The same is true in novels. Stories tell us who people are and what they're doing. By filling in the backdrop to the action, your reader's understanding of events is expanded and enhanced. Readers must see your characters and the choices they're making in a context, and that context can change the way they will judge them or relate to them.

To illustrate this point, imagine a teenage boy walking down a road. Although he is tall and muscular, he looks nervous, glancing over his shoulder and jumping at every sound. Without a setting in place, that teen might be scared or guilty. He might be brave or he might be a coward. The scene might be serious or humorous.

Now add in certain details that allow us to see the picture clearer. It's nighttime and the boy has a book under his arm. A book of ghost stories. The road is a worn path through the woods. Owls hoot and tree limbs make dark shadows on the path. The teen is wearing an Eagle Scout uniform and walking toward a campfire far in the distance.

Several younger Boy Scouts are snickering as they walk behind him. They don't seem at all afraid, while he jumps at every sound.

Do you see how the story gradually emerges?

Now imagine a different setting for the same boy. This time he's walking down a city street. Burned-out buildings rise up around him as he hurries along. It's just getting dark and there are people in the background—gangs of teenagers huddled together, emphasizing the boy's isolation. A car alarm sounds in the distance and police sirens are heard. The stink of garbage rises up from a gutter. The boy's eyes flicker to two people making a drug deal, and then he turns his gaze straight ahead, focusing on the one apartment building in the distance that he calls home.

This scene could play out in any number of ways—always substituting the generic "road" for something more specific—but whichever choices you make, the setting is helping the reader to set her expectations of both the character and the action that might follow. Offering your reader clues as to what kind of book you're writing is important, so you'll want to choose a setting that enhances your reader's understanding not only of what's already happening, but also what's about to happen. Once you've established the basics—time and place—you'll be able to use sensory details to develop your chosen environment until it seems as real to the reader as any place he's ever been.

CHOOSING A TIME PERIOD

When someone says the word "setting" in the context of writing, the first thing that jumps to most people's minds is *where* a book takes place. We'll be discussing locations next, but before we do, let's look at an aspect of setting that's often overlooked.

Not where, but *when*.

Many people outside the field of YA literature mistakenly associate writing for teens with writing contemporary fiction. The stereotype of the YA novel is a first-person narrative set in a modern-day school, and the stereotype of the YA novelist is someone who is constantly fighting to stay on top of the trends so her books won't seem outdated.

Of course, as we learned in third period, there can be some truth to stereotypes, and many YA novels do take place in modern-day settings. They might very well feature characters who need to fit into these settings by wearing the right clothes, using the newest technology, and speaking with the latest slang words. But this is only a small part of what's open to the author of teen literature. Just as Social Studies class in school didn't focus solely on modern American history, the smart YA writer opens her field of possibilities to include every place and time period in history and beyond.

Take a look at books like *The Braid* by Helen Frost, *Feed* by M.T. Anderson, and *A Great and Terrible Beauty* by Libba Bray and you will see that literature for young adults is open to being set in any place and time an author can dream up.

So how can you choose the best time period for your book? Usually the time period of your novel will come along with the idea itself. It's rare that events would lend themselves equally well to historical fiction, modern day, and fantasy or science fiction. Generally, when you get an idea you'll also get some sense of a character to go along with it, and that character will have a specific story to tell. How she speaks and what she says will be the largest influences on which time period you'll choose. Do you hear an old-fashioned voice or a futuristic one? Does the story itself fit naturally into a specific historical time period or would that constrain the action, imposing limitations that would be difficult to work with?

When you choose a time period you must be careful to work within the boundaries that the time imposes. For example, you might want to create a female character who takes a leadership role in your story. Depending on when your book takes place, this might be more or less of a challenge. Although your underlying desire might be to show your character's strength, which is a timeless quality, if you set the book in the distant past you might need to find inventive ways of accomplishing this goal in order to avoid stretching your reader's believability to the breaking point. Or if you decide to have your character take on a nontraditional role, be sure the opposition facing her is true to what it would have been during that particular time.

If your book is set in the future, or another imaginary time or place, you set the boundaries for your characters. This might seem simple at first glance, but it's essential to be consistent throughout your story, not allowing the rules of the society you've created to shift as the story progresses. It's also important to give your imaginary time period a multidimensional quality, alluding to what has come before and what might be in store in the future. For some people, this kind of detailed creation of another world will be appealing, but for others it might be far more work than they bargained for.

Always assess your own strengths as a writer when you choose which time period your story is best suited for. Historical fiction involves a lot of research, and the details you include must not only be accurate, they must also be purposeful—chosen to advance the plot rather than to show off your knowledge of the era. Is this kind of thorough research something you'd enjoy? Do you have firsthand knowledge of the time period you'd like to use for your setting?

Writing & Selling the *ya novel*

If your answer to that last question is "yes," you still need to check your facts. Even if you grew up in the 1960s or 1970s, would your recollections be accurate? Might you remember a certain historical event as having happened at one point when it really happened at another? Did that sports team win the championship in 1986 or 1987? What year did that hurricane hit? Small details can make or break your portrayal of a time period. You not only have to get the facts right, but you also have to get the fashions, politics, attitudes, and entertainments correct.

Think of everything that defines our current era and make those same things relevant in whatever time you're writing about— even if that time period is made up. Part of what makes fantasy and science fiction as popular as they are today is the level of attention given to creating the worlds that the characters operate in. So many of these books are parts of series, and I imagine some of the reasoning behind this is that the worlds themselves often take on lives of their own. They're so real to us that we want to explore them far beyond the pages of just one book. The best science fiction delves into the future as accurately as historical fiction delves into the past.

Is this where your strength as a writer lies?

Another consideration when choosing a time period is how your setting might affect your plot. Remember that strong female protagonist? How does she change as we move her around in history? What kinds of obstacles will she meet in 1694 as opposed to 1964? Should you show her standing up to injustice and fighting for her rights? Or could you contrast her character better in a futuristic setting where young women have forgotten the lessons of the past, becoming soft and lazy, and deliberately allowing men to dominate?

Choosing a time period that's unexpected is like moving a light from one side of the room to another. It casts different shadows. A time period outside of a modern-day setting can wake a reader up and force him to see familiar things in a new way. Just be sure you do everything in your power to capture the spirit and facts of the times.

Factors to Consider When Choosing Your Time Period

Education systems: How does your time period and location affect who has access to different types of education? Even in a modern-day setting, consider carefully what type of school an inner-city student might attend versus a student in the rural Midwest.

Speech patterns: The way we speak changes from location to location, but also from time period to time period. Choose your slang wisely, but also be aware of what words and subjects might be taboo.

Attitudes and prejudices: Just as speech patterns change, so do attitudes and prejudices. We are all affected by when and where we live. Writing YA gives you a great opportunity to create teen characters who question these popular assumptions.

Politics: What kind of political system is in place and how do teenagers fit into it? Do they have any power or influence? How does the political climate affect your character (even if he or she is unaware of the effect)?

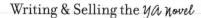

Fashion: What are teens wearing and how do the fashions of the times reflect society? Are clothes modest or provocative? How does your teen character feel about his wardrobe?

Fads and entertainments: The way a society chooses to entertain itself says a lot about its values. What's popular in your character's world? How does he or she relax and have fun?

Important figures: Who are the people who shape your character's life and the society they live in? Are they celebrities? Parents? Teachers? Historical figures? Scientists? Know who your character looks up to and who they despise.

Foods and famines: What kind of cuisine is present in your setting? Is food plentiful or scarce? Spicy or bland? How is food eaten? Are meals social or solitary?

Religion: What are the religious beliefs of the day and how does your teen character feel about them? What does their participation or lack of participation in organized religion tell the reader about who they are as a person?

Wars and conflicts: What's going on in your character's world that's notable? Even fictionalized worlds need to have a three dimensional quality, and giving your reader a sense of ongoing historical events can make your setting more believable.

Scientific beliefs: Scientific beliefs change with the times, and knowing what the people within a certain setting believe to be true is more important than what you personally believe is true. Make sure your science is consistent with your setting.

Role of teenagers: In every one of these categories, consider where teenagers fit in. Think about how teens in general would feel about each subject, and then think about how your specific teen character would relate. Do they fall in line with their peers? How does the society you're portraying view teens?

Weather: Different times in history have been marked by significant storms and weather patterns. It would be hard to set a book in 2005 without mentioning Hurricane Katrina. Even in futuristic novels you can use the weather to create a distinct mood and make your setting come to life.

Even if you do choose a modern-day setting, take equal pains to illuminate the world around your characters. Don't assume your reader will have the same context that you do for interpreting our times. Just because we all live in the 2000s doesn't mean our settings have much else in common. 2010 in Beverly Hills will look very different from 2010 in inner-city New Orleans. Remember that setting a story in a modern time period is not an excuse to take setting for granted. Instead, it's a chance to make our "familiar" world all the more vivid to your readers.

LOCATION

Let's pull down that world map again. Okay, now take out a thumbtack and close your eyes. I'll point you in the right direction and then … Wait! Surely there's a better way to choose a location for your story.

Of course there is. Just as choosing a time period for your teen novel is more involved than defaulting to modern day, selecting and portraying where you'd like your book to take place is more complicated than pinning the proverbial thumbtack onto a map. Possible locations are infinite, since they can be real or imaginary, urban or rural. They can draw on what's familiar or play on what's unfamiliar. The scope of your setting might be broad or narrow, depending on what you're trying to accomplish, and most times, several locations will be used during the course of one novel. This means it's your job as the author to develop each place the character goes until it's multidimensional.

Take, for example, a novel set in New York City. Within this urban environment, you might also establish specific locations like your character's school, apartment, and wherever he relaxes. Maybe your character spends a lot of time on the subway, so the subway cars themselves become a location within a location. Or perhaps he takes trips out of the city on the weekends into rural Hudson Valley. The more locations you include, the more time you need to spend developing these worlds. So what are the characteristics of locations? A good place to start is by using your five senses.

Locations have sights.

Locations have sounds.

Locations have smells.

Locations have textures.

Locations have tastes.

Wait a minute! Tastes? How can you taste a location? Maybe this seems like a stretch, but if you think about it, you'll realize that the foods we eat play a huge part in defining our culture. You can't write about New Orleans without including red beans and rice and jambalaya. And Maine would be lacking without lobster and clams. Locations several continents away can come alive when you describe local cuisines like curried goat or spicy flatbread.

Beyond regional foods, I would suggest that certain locations also have tastes associated with the places themselves, like standing on the seashore and tasting the salt on the wind or in the surf. How about the acrid taste of smoke or the way thirst dries out the tongue, obliterating all but the taste of desire?

Every one of our senses plays a part in describing a setting for your reader. What do the characters see in every scene? Sometimes sights will be vast, like the horizon seen from a sailing ship, but other times what a character sees can be very limited and mundane—and that's okay! Settings don't have to be spectacular to be well drawn; they only have to work for your book.

Imagine a setting as limited as a padded room in an institution. Your character will see the same thing day after day, but that monotony can allow the reader to experience part of what it means to be imprisoned. And when one sense is limited, you have the possibility of using another sense to a fuller degree. Perhaps the teen in the institution can hear things happening outside her room. Hushed conversations between doctors and nurses. An alarm that sounds. The crash of something metallic being overturned and clattering to the floor. By using sounds more than sights, you can create a sense of bewilderment or anxiety as they place the reader outside the comfort zone of what's familiar.

Smell is also an important part of location. There's nothing that brings memory back as powerfully as our sense of smell. When a character moves through different settings, this power can be harnessed to make the location vivid. As the reader remembers the smells you are describing, the emotions associated with them are apt to follow.

Here's a short passage from *Hush* by Jacqueline Woodson:

Writing & Selling the *ya novel*

> Later, with the coconut cake still resting in her stom-
> ach, the youngest rises from her bed and stares into
> the night—the moon is bright yellow, the sky is blue-
> black, the shadows that are the Rocky Mountains. She
> sniffs, inhaling the scent of pine and cedar and air that
> is warm still—but with winter at its edges.

Do you find this description of the air to be as evocative as I do? In-stantly, I am transported to places and times when I have smelled the first hints of crisp winter cold on the breeze. I remember the mixed emotions that came with it: excitement and a growing ten-sion associated with coming change. The addition of smell loads the scene with expectation.

How about texture? What does our sense of touch add to the de-scription of a location? Places can be hot and cold. They can feel gritty or soft or smooth. Imagine the textures inherent in locations such as a beach, a grassy field, a high school biology room, or a swimming pool. There will be many different textures in every location, and it's the writer's job to choose which ones her characters interact with.

In fact, with every single aspect of setting, there are choices that need to be made. Benjamin N. Cardozo said, "There is an accuracy that defeats itself by the overemphasis of details." What he's referring to is the tendency to want to tell the reader everything so we can rec-reate the exact same picture in his head that exists in our own mind, but this is an impossibility. Every reader will bring his unique ex-periences to your book and will imagine things in different ways. By failing to make choices about which information to include, we can overwhelm our readers with a recitation of facts, and the story itself can get buried under plodding, though poetic, descriptions.

Details are important—every sense into our setting can bring a story to life—but making judgment calls about what to say and when is what being a writer is all about. Choose the information that best advances the plot, sheds light on your characters, or sets the tone.

Teen Panel

DO YOU Prefer BOOKS THAT TAKE PLACE IN A WORLD SIMILAR TO YOUR OWN WORLD TO BOOKS THAT TAKE PLACE IN OTHER TIME PERIODS/WORLDS/ENVIRONMENTS? WHAT MAKES AN UNFAMILIAR SETTING INTERESTING TO YOU?

(Author's Note: Of those surveyed, the responses to this question were split almost equally three ways; those who preferred similar settings slightly outnumbered those who preferred fantasy settings and those who said they liked both settings.)

Caylynn, age 13, California: I like other time periods, worlds, and environments. When I read a really good book in a mythical land, I feel like I'm there. I'm the character in the rain or a scary situation.

Katherine, age 16, New Mexico: I prefer books to take place in our world. I find unfamiliar settings interesting only if very detailed.

Tori, age 17, British Columbia, Canada: I like both familiar and unfamiliar settings, as long as they are shown realistically. A book set in Wisconsin can be less believable than one set in a fantasy setting if the fantasy setting is depicted better. As long as there are ties here and there to the "real world" (even if it's something like realistic dynamics between friends, rather than all acting in the same medieval way to-wards each other), I think either type of setting can be enjoyable.

Marco, age 15, New Mexico: I prefer books to be closer to home because then you're able to relate more to the environment and time period. Unfamiliar settings sometimes take longer to get used to be-cause they are so unfamiliar.

David, age 14, New Mexico: I think it's cool to read a novel that takes place somewhere else because, by reading, you can put your feet in their shoes.

Sirena, age 15, New Mexico: I prefer books written within one hun-dred years of my time. When I can relate things to that I know, I have better understanding and will be more interested.

USING SETTING TO CREATE TONE

Creating tone and developing setting go hand-in-hand. Remember what I said earlier about giving your reader clues as to what kind of story you're telling? Well, one of the best ways to do that is by setting the tone of your book from page one. We've all heard the cliché open-ing line, "It was a dark and stormy night." Sometimes clichés exist for a reason. This first line has probably been overused in part because it works so well. From the very first sentence the mood is established.

Take a look at these other openings and see what kind of tone is established for each book. This one's from *Are You in the House Alone?*, by Richard Peck:

> For that first warm night of spring until autumn,
> Steve and I would slip out to the Pastorinis' cottage
> on the lake, Powdermill Lake. How often? Ten times?
> Twelve? I don't remember now. I kept no diary. We
> left no clues.

Immediately we sense there is something elicit going on in this story. The image of warm summer nights predominates, and within these few lines I already have a picture of an empty cottage on a lake—someplace remote. The movement from the generic "lake" to the specific "Powdermill Lake" makes it seem as if perhaps we might have heard of this place. In the news, maybe? Combine that with the last line, "We left no clues," and a sense of trouble begins to creep up your spine. The mood is set.

How about this passage from Julia DeVillers's *How My Private, Personal Journal Became a Bestseller*:

> "Thirty seconds! Thirty seconds until showtime, everyone!!"
>
> I shifted around, trying to get comfortable. You'd think a TV talk show would have a comfortable chair for their guests. I mean, some of the hugest celebrities in the world had sat on this exact chair. And they were probably not comfortable, either.

Here we have an entirely different tone being set—excitement. There's urgency and a thrill to the opening dialogue, but then the uncomfortable chair sets the reader slightly on edge. Not the type of edge that a story about a murder would inspire, but enough that we're nervous for the main character though we've barely met her. We expect something big to happen because she's on national TV, but we don't necessarily think things are going to go smoothly.

Here's the beautiful opening of An Na's poetic novel *A Step From Heaven*:

> Just to the edge, Young Ju. Only your feet. Stay there.
>
> Cold. Cold water. Oh. My toes are fish. Come here. Fast. Look.
>
> What is it, Young Ju?
>
> See my toes. See how they are swimming in the sea? Like fish.
>
> Yes, they are little fat piggy fish.
>
> Ahhh! Tickles.
>
> Come on. Up. Keep your legs around me. Are you ready to go swim in the waves?
>
> Hold me. Hold me.
>
> I have you. Look over there, Young Ju. See how the waves dance. See? Hold on tight. We are going over there.
>
> No. Stop. Deep water. Go back.
>
> Shhh, Young Ju. Do not be afraid. You must learn how to be brave. See, I have you.

What a wonderful use of setting to create both a nostalgic tone and fore-shadowing. Right away, as we look out over the ocean, there is a sense of a long journey about to be taken. The little girl's apprehension about the waves, along with the father's warning to be brave, suggest that the journey will be difficult. Details like the cold water tickling her feet make the scene vivid and real, and we have a sense that perhaps the narrator is looking back wistfully to an easier time when she felt safe and loved.

See how these authors' varied choices of location and the details they chose to provide lend themselves to fabulous setups? I chose those examples because each of them made me want to keep reading, hooking me with a mood of anticipation and using tone to suggest the future course of the book.

Tone is a powerful manipulator of the human spirit. Think how great an effect our tone of voice can have on a listener in real life. When you set a strong mood, you're accomplishing the same thing. When the tone is one the reader enjoys experiencing, even if that experience is fear or horror, she will seek out your book and return to it again and again.

Let's take a look at one last novel. Susan Cooper is one of the great masters of mood. She uses well-chosen details of sight, sound, smell, touch, and taste to draw readers in until they are so thoroughly enveloped in the world she's creating that they don't want to leave. I can still vividly recall reading this series aloud with my family when I was young. I remember curling up in the windowsill watching the dark shadows of the tree branches bending and weaving outside, shivering as my father's voice brought Cooper's world to life.

Here are just a few ways *The Dark Is Rising*, the first book in her award-winning series, sets the tension-filled mood that pervades the novel. The book opens with a crowded household where too many brothers and sisters jostle for position. We're on the Dawson's farm, and outside, "All the broad sky was gray, full of more snow that refused to fall. There was no colour anywhere." It's four days until Christmas. The loud bustle of activity in the household is punctuated by the screech of static as the main character passes by the radio on the kitchen table. Will and his brother go outside to the "farm-smelling barn" to feed their rabbits, and find them "restless and uneasy."

The rooks call relentlessly overhead. Walking to a neighbor's house Will sees a strange-looking, hunched-over man who "scuttled, like a beetle." The clouds grow darker, "massing in ominous grey mounds with a yellowish tinge," and the wind "rises, stirring their hair."

Can you feel the heaviness of the impending action? Cooper uses every sense to create a tone that's ominous. She contrasts the warm images of hearth light, Christmas, and the taste of fresh-baked bread with the cold gray blanket smothering the outside world. Right from the start we sense something unnatural is happening. The static from the radio, the strange behavior of the weather and the animals, the odd sighting of the hunched man … Like the main character, Will, we become jumpy, anticipating what will come next.

Notice, as well, that it was impossible for me to quote her descriptions in block. Good writers disperse details throughout the text, allowing them to subtly work their magic even as the reader is distracted by the action and dialogue. Sometimes the setting is even revealed *through* the dialogue and action.

Here's part of the conversation the two boys have about the restless rabbits:

> "Hey!" Will said, disturbed. "Hey, James, look at that. What's the matter with him? And all of them?"
>
> "They seem all right to me."
>
> "Well, they don't to me. They're all jumpy. Even Chelsea. …"

Although we've never seen these particular rabbits, we get a sense of the strangeness of their behavior through Will's reaction. When Will catches a glimpse of the hunched-over man, he jumps, clutching his brother's arm. The details are everywhere, so well integrated into the action, that they're impossible to remove without destroying the story. This is a sure sign of setting done right.

You, too, can create a strong setting and use it to enhance your plot. Just imagine the world not only as your character sees it, but also as he smells it, touches it, hears it, and tastes it. Remember that teens are still discovering the world, so don't forget to include that sense of awe and newness that can pervade the teenage years. Let your character's worldview shape the way you portray your setting, and in turn, your setting will shape your reader's view of the world you've created.

Homework: Choose one of the ideas you developed in 2nd Period and explored further in 3rd Period English. Now try experimenting with setting instead of character or plot. Write two different scenes featuring your chosen protagonist acting out the scenario you've selected, but this time choose starkly different locations and/ or time periods to see how they affect the plot. See if you can set a tone for each scene that hints at what's to come.

Here's an example: Let's say that earlier you worked on developing the idea of a male student who has a crush on his football coach. You could now write two scenes—one that takes place in a poor inner-city school where football is barely funded and therefore the coach is desperate for every player he can get, and another that takes place in a rich suburban environment where the football team always has the best, cleanest, newest equipment and the role of football player is reserved for the school's elite. You could choose a modern time period in which homosexuality is not as hidden as it was in the past, or you could choose to set the scene in the 1950s when it was rarely acknowledged.

Each choice will lead to different ramifications for your character and plot. Will your main character have to fight hard for a spot on the team? How does he feel about his crush on the coach? Will the tone of the story be tragic or comic?

See how developing different settings can enhance your writing and shed new light on your characters and the choices they make.

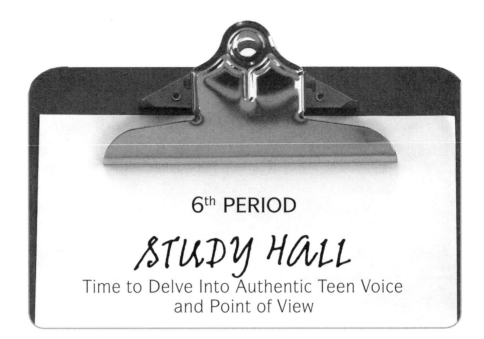

6th PERIOD

STUDY HALL

Time to Delve Into Authentic Teen Voice
and Point of View

When I was in school, study hall was seldom an occasion for actual studying. More often than not it was a time to pass notes, talk with friends, or make some excuse to skip out for makeup gym classes. Often it was when I got my homework done for the class ahead if I hadn't done it the night before. Still, there were times—like just before a big test—that studying really *did* happen, and we're going to pretend this is one of those times.

Imagine the test you're about to take is on narrative voice and points of view.

Why devote an entire chapter to voice? Well, for years YA novels have been known for their unique narrative voices and teenage perspectives. Regardless of whether these characteristics are true for *every* teen novel, voice and point of view are worth looking into and understanding fully. When used well, both can distinguish your work, allowing you to capture characters, events, and settings in a way that's integral to your narrator's way of seeing her world. Developing a convincing teen voice for your characters takes a lot of time, patience, and practice, but fortunately we've got a whole period devoted to studying.

WHAT IS NARRATIVE VOICE?

Every person, fictional or real, has a way of speaking that is uniquely his own. We touched upon voice in English class when we discussed a character's speech as something that can distinguish her from another person. Our word choices and speech patterns reveal who we are, where we're from, and what we're thinking. They can make us interesting or dull, aggravating or sympathetic.

The same is true for narrative voice. Your narrator can be revealed by what he chooses to say and how he says it. When one of your characters is telling the story, narrative voice can be a form of character development. Other times, the narrator might be more removed—someone outside the story looking in. Her voice might be very different from that of the characters she's describing. The narrator might be a teen who is judgmental or reflective. He might also be an adult looking back on his youth—the voice of experience commenting on his past journey.

Narrative voices have distinctive speech patterns and tones, as well. They can be authoritative or questioning, and this can involve the reader, drawing her in, or distance the reader, keeping her at arm's length. The narrator can tell the story from the past or present, and at times he might even be imagining, or speaking from, the future. There can be multiple narrators for the same story, and they can each relate the same events from different perspectives, or they can slowly advance the plot by adding pieces of the story that only they know.

When it comes to narrative voice, your options are endless. You'll want to be aware of them, but don't let the scope of the choices overwhelm you. Stripped down to its most basic, what a narrative voice needs to establish is:

- who is telling the story
- what her relationship is to the events unfolding

For an easy frame of reference, think of your friends and family. How would each of them tell other people about the same event? Do you have an aunt who makes everything sound hilarious, always sprinkling jokes into monologues worthy of a comedy club? Do you have a friend who turns everything into high drama? Or a sister who can make any situation seem primed for romance? What about that cousin who never reveals any emotion, always leaving you to guess what's really going on inside his head?

That's the "who" of narrative voice. Depending on who the narrator is, she brings her own personal style to the telling of the story.

Here's an example of an exceptional narrative voice from *The Perks of Being a Wallflower* by Stephen Chbosky. Charlie tells the story in a series of letters to an anonymous friend, and this is how it begins:

> Dear friend,
>
> I am writing to you because she said you listen and understand and didn't try to sleep with that person at the party even though you could have. Please don't try to figure out who she is, because then you might figure out who I am, and I really don't want you to do

that. I will call people by different names or generic names because I don't want you to find me. I didn't enclose a return address for the same reason. I mean nothing bad by this. Honest.

I just need to know that someone out there listens and understands and doesn't try to sleep with people even if they could have. I need to know that these people exist.

I think you of all people would understand that because I think that you of all people are alive and appreciate what that means. At least, I hope you do because other people look to you for strength and friendship, and it's that simple. At least that's what I've heard.

So, this is my life. And I want you to know that I am both happy and sad and I'm still trying to figure out how that could be.

Do you have an immediate sense of Charlie's character even though he's trying to hide his identity? The narrative voice is so effective that even while you know nothing of what Charlie looks like, where he's from, how old he is, or who he's addressing, you understand certain key parts of his personality, such as his vulnerability and idealism, and his intense longing for a world that's fair and just.

Here's another example of narrative voice in action from Justina Chen Headley's *Nothing But the Truth (and a few white lies):*

Abe got eighty percent of the Mama-looking genes in our family; I got the dregs. There is no mistaking whose son Abe is with his jet-black hair, high cheekbones, and flat rice cake of a butt. Take a look at any

> Ho family picture and guess which one doesn't look like the others? Hint: the gawky girl with brownish hair and large eyes with a natural fold that Korean girls have surgically created. It's as if God cruised through one of those Chinese fast-food buffets and bought Abe the full meal deal so he can pass for Mama's beloved son. When it came to my turn, all that was left was one of those soggy egg rolls that doesn't qualify as real Chinese food.

This is an entirely different character, and her voice is accordingly unique. She sees the world and relates to the reader in a wholly different manner. For Patty Ho, how she looks and where she comes from are essential to her identity.

Narrators are as diverse as real people, and the information they decide to hide or impart is one way we get to know them. The better we know them, the more easily we can interpret the action of the story because we understand how they see the world and how they relate to events in the story. Ask yourself about your narrator's relationship to the action.

- Is he an observer?
- Is he a participant?
- Is he telling us something he only heard about or imagined?

Each of these choices lends to or detracts from his credibility, and each choice will change the way we understand what's taking place.

Remember that aunt who makes everything sound hilarious? Well, maybe the family fight wouldn't have been so funny if she'd been directly involved in it. If you know her well, you would probably listen to her story knowing it wasn't really the laugh riot she's making it out to be. Perhaps your sister can conjure up a romantic glow for every occasion in part because she chooses to use her imagination to enhance reality. Maybe she relates more of what she hears from others than what she experiences herself, and since you understand where she's coming from, you can see through the rosy haze to the loneliness underneath.

Here's one more example of narrative voice from one of the masters of narration, Robert Cormier. Watch how he puts his own unique spin on something very familiar—a football team tryout—in his classic *The Chocolate War.*

> They murdered him.
>
> As he turned to take the ball, a dam burst against the side of his head and a hand grenade shattered his stomach. Engulfed by nausea, he pitched toward the grass. His mouth encountered gravel, and he spit frantically, afraid that some of his teeth had been knocked out. Rising to his feet he saw the field through drifting gauze but held on until everything settled into place, like a lens focusing, making the world sharp again, with edges.
>
> The second play called for a pass. Fading back, he picked up a decent block and cocked his arm, searching for a receiver—maybe the tall kid they called The Goober. Suddenly he was caught from behind and whirled violently, a toy boat caught in a whirlpool. Landing on his knees, hugging the ball, he urged himself to ignore the pain that gripped his groin, knowing that it was important to betray no sign of distress,

remembering The Goober's advice, "Coach is testing you, testing, and he's looking for guts."

Would another narrator tell this story differently? You bet. This is a narrator who is watching and judging. He pulls no punches, right from the very first line, and he sees murder lurking in something you and I would accept as commonplace.

This is the power of narrative voice—to show us the world through someone else's eyes. Someone who is, perhaps, completely unlike us. Narrators can disappear from the page, or they can "become" the story. Regardless, it's important to establish the tone and the narrator's relationship to the action right from the first page of your book and to be consistent with that choice throughout your novel.

POINT OF VIEW

To learn how to establish a narrator's relationship to events, let's take a closer look at point of view. If narrative voice is how a narrator tells the story in terms of tone and emotion, point of view is the perspective from which she tells it. The two go hand in hand. Perspective will shape tone, and tone will shape perspective.

The same two questions above apply here as well. Who is telling the story, and what is his relationship to the unfolding events? The answer can come in several forms.

- **First person:** The narrator is an eyewitness to events; she tells the story from her own perspective, using the "I" voice.

- **Second person:** You are the star of the show, and the narrator's role is to relate what "you" are doing and saying, using the "you" voice.

- **Third person:** The narrator is telling about something that happened to someone else, using the "he/she" voice.

- **Omniscient:** The narrator is godlike, unlimited in his ability to know what many characters are thinking and doing.

In addition to point of view, there's also the issue of tense—is the narrator telling the story using past, present, or future tense?

- **Past tense:** Events have already happened, and the narrator is looking back on them.

- **Present:** Events are presented as if they are happening now.

- **Future:** The narrator exists in the present, but events are happening in the imagined future

Just using these two very short lists, you can probably guess which points of view and which tenses are used more frequently and which ones might present difficulties. Anyone want to tackle second person, future tense? Probably not. You'll find some narrative techniques lend themselves more easily to a natural, rhythmic writing style. Still, every story is different, and you never know when you'll want to try a point of view you've never used before, so it's worth exploring all of your options in more depth.

FIRST-PERSON POINT OF VIEW

Let's start by taking a closer look at first person. This is one of the most common points of view in teen fiction. In fact, when most people think of books written for young adults, this is the point of view they often assume the book is written in.

Why? First person is conversational. The character is talking directly to the reader, so right from the start the reader and the character have an implied relationship. This relationship might be one where the reader takes on the role of confidant, such as in Julia DeVillers's *How My Private, Personal Journal Became a Bestseller*, where the narrator makes the reader part of the action by assuming you've read her best-selling journal-turned-book and seen the publicity surrounding it. She then goes on to give the reader the inside scoop about what was really happening.

Or it might be a more distant relationship such as the one presented in Walter Dean Myers's *Monster*, where the reader is the imagined audience for the narrator's screenplay—an audience that will ultimately judge him for his actions. Regardless, in first person, the narrating character and the reader connect, and this makes first person feel intimate. The reader is up close and personal with the action in the story.

FIRST PERSON, PAST TENSE

Let's look at several versions of the same short passage—a simple scene in which a character's luck turns bad—ominously bad—all written in first person, past tense.

Version one:

> I can't tell you when I first knew I was in trouble. It was probably the day I found the note stuffed in my locker. It was tattered, as if the person who'd put it there had difficulty getting it through the slots. I still remember the way I picked it up so casually, still completely naive about what was to come. If I'd known then what I know now, I would have stuffed it back inside. But instead, I read it.

I know all your secrets.

Who would have written that? It couldn't have any-thing to do with ...

I looked around, searching desperately for some-one lingering nearby, laughing at their own stupid joke, but the hallway was empty. Eerily empty. Suddenly, I was all alone.

In this passage, the narrator is the person at the center of the ac-tion and he's relating things that have already happened in the past. First person, past tense. We hear his thoughts and observe all the events through his viewpoint. Might he be lying to us? Yes, this is a possibility, and depending on what type of book you're writing, this lingering possibility can be used to your advantage. In the pas-sage above, does the character seem like a good guy, or is he per-haps guilty of some crime? Even though he's telling the story, we don't know for certain, and this tension could easily be played out through the rest of the novel.

Still, we're inclined to be sympathetic. Why exactly is this? Be-cause he's confiding his inner most thoughts and feelings, so we identify with his point of view, not someone else's. It's rare for a per-son to cast himself in a bad light, so if the narrator is, in fact, a bad guy, we will most likely have to pick up that fact through the actions we see him take. Otherwise, we'll be hearing his version of events despite the fact that someone else might have related everything quite differently.

Now let's see how that same scenario might look presented by some-one who is still involved in the action, but slightly more removed.

Version two:

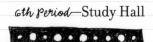

I can't tell you when I first knew Jeff was in trouble. It was probably the day he found the note stuffed in his locker. I remember the way he took it out so casually, still laughing about the joke he'd been telling. The note was tattered, as if the person who'd put it there had difficulty getting it through the slots, and I wondered if it might be from Allie. Then Jeff's face went as white as the snow blanketing the school yard. He looked around wildly, as if someone might be hiding around the corner with a huge knife or something.

"What's wrong?" I asked.

He shook his head and shoved the note in his pocket. "Nothing," he said, turning away and striding down the hall.

If I'd known then what I know now, I never would have accepted that answer.

This is still first-person narration. It's still past tense. Everything is still being filtered through the eyes of the narrator, only now the reader has the sense that the action will really center around Jeff and the narrator is an observer—involved, but not as closely involved as in version one.

It's important to note the distinction between this type of first person and third person, because the two can easily be confused. Here, the narrator is telling us about what happened to someone else (which we will see again when we use third-person narration) but the events are being filtered through his life and his point of view. For example, what happens to Jeff once he disappears down the hallway? Since the narrator is no longer with him, we don't know. They could have a conversation about it later on, or the narrator might speculate, but the reader only sees what the narrator has access to. The same is true for thoughts and feelings about the events that take place. The narrator can tell us how *he* felt, and he can tell us how Jeff looked, or how he *thinks* Jeff might have felt, but he cannot jump inside Jeff's head and share his actual emotions.

This is one of the most common mistakes in manuscripts, and it's referred to as a point-of-view shift. Writers must be consistent with whichever point of view they choose, and that means accepting the limitations that come with it. If I choose to write my first-person narrative from the friend's point of view rather than Jeff's, the friend can't know definitively what's going on in Jeff's mind, or what Jeff does when out of sight. He can only make educated guesses or relate the information that he hears from Jeff or from others.

FIRST PERSON, PRESENT TENSE

Let's look at one last example of first-person narration, only this time let's play with tense instead of perspective. What would this passage look like if it were told in present tense instead of past tense?

Version three:

> I'm standing at my locker, taking out my books and thinking about Allie Carter's amazingly long legs when a note falls out onto the floor.
>
> Just like that.
>
> There's no fanfare. No warning. In fact, as I lean down to pick it up, I'm still grinning, thinking it might be from Allie, but then I see the words scrawled across the crumpled page.
>
> *I know all your secrets.*

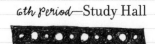

I squint, confused, and look around. This has got to be a joke, right? Except no one's peering around the corner ready to point and laugh. In fact, the hallway is empty now. Eerily empty. Suddenly I'm all alone.

In this version, we've still got the same basic plot, but the details change as the point of view and the tense shift. We get a slightly different look at what is happening. The tone is more immediate now in the present tense, so there's an urgency to the narration, but we've lost some of the ominous tone that can come when the narrator has foreknowledge of events and can hint at what's about to happen.

With each choice you make there are trade-offs—limitations, but also advantages. Don't be afraid to experiment with different points of view and different tenses to see which combination works best for you and your story. Even if you know you want to use first-person narration, you still have a lot of options available.

I will offer a couple words of warning about first person before we move on. While the first-person point of view is great for drawing the reader in and revealing your character's personality, it's also easy to write sloppily while using it. Even when the narrator is telling about what happened to her, not every sentence can begin with I, and dialogue and actions must still be your primary tools for advancing the plot. The danger of first person is that it can lull you into complacency with whichever voice you are using to narrate. Why show a conversation when the narrator can just tell the reader all about what happened using his oh-so-witty narrative voice? But you'll find that even the most clever, articulate, or funny narrative voices wear thin when that's all we hear page after page. Even when using first person, the old adage "show, don't tell" still applies!

WHAT MAKES A TEEN VOICE IN A NOVEL SOUND FAKE?

(Author's Note: The most common response to this question had to do with an author's use of language—either an improper use of slang, or trying too hard to sound like a teen and not pulling it off. The other answers that came up again and again were when authors use stereotypes and when authors overexaggerate.)

Shelby, age 16, Michigan: The thing that really makes a teen character unrealistic is when everything in his/her life is either perfect or terrible. I have yet to meet someone who hates or loves every part of their life. Even extremely depressed people find some enjoyment in their lives.

Tori, age 17, British Columbia, Canada: When it's inconsistent. I don't have a problem with teens using big words or talking in monosyllables, as long as they don't go from saying "Excellent" to "Coolio" in two pages. Also, unless there's a reason for it (i.e. the narrator is an adult looking back on their teenage life, or life experience merits it) a worldly, all-knowing narrator can be a not-so-subtle reminder that it's an adult writing the book, not a teenager narrating it.

Chaunter, age 15, New Mexico: When they overexaggerate on things. The things I exaggerate most are homework and guys, same as most of my friends. We also joke about drugs and sex a bunch, but we don't really do anything!

Emily, age 17, Michigan: When the novel is saying what happened but there's no emotion in what the character is trying to say.

Salvador, age 14, New Mexico: A teen voice sounds fake in a novel when it sounds respectful, fluent, and if he uses long, difficult words.

Ilana, age 17, Florida: Misuse of slang. Simplification of the weight of the issues we face today—and then overdramatizing the weight of things that are not issues today. Not providing a background to an issue. Making a character one-dimensional—like he'll have goals and ambitions, but no general reason why he has these goals and ambitions.

Cala, age 16, Michigan: I think they sound fake when they have really good grammar and they're way too nice.

Karsten, age 15, New Mexico: Trying to "talk like a gangsta, dawg." Teens don't all talk like that!

THIRD-PERSON AND OMNISCIENT POINTS OF VIEW

For the moment, let's skip over second-person point of view and take a more in-depth look at third-person and omniscient points of view, which actually overlap since third person is a form of the omniscient viewpoint.

Let's begin by studying third person. This is the "he/she" voice where the narrator is outside of the events of the story, telling us about what happened to someone else. We see third-person narrative often in novels, and it's a technique that works well for telling almost any type of story. Third-person narration is very versatile, and while it might sometimes lack the conversational tone of first person, it can be an exceptional point of view to use when you're looking to create a distinct mood or tone for your book. It can offer the writer plenty of ways to convey information without the limitations of what the narrator alone would tell us.

Let's take a look at that same passage from before, now written in third person. Watch how the text changes as the point of view shifts.

Version four:

> The day Jeff found the note in his locker was one of the worst days he'd ever had—it was even worse than the day his parents announced their divorce. In fact, up until the moment the crumpled note fell onto his sneaker and he smoothed out the paper in order to read the scrawled words, he hadn't known that days could get so bad.
>
> Or so dangerous.
>
> Jeff squinted at the words on the page.
>
> *I know all your secrets.*
>
> They couldn't possibly mean what he thought they meant. Or could they? He looked up, glancing around the hallway for someone nearby—some practical joker, ready to say, "You should have seen your face!" But there was no one. The hallway was empty.
>
> Had he missed the bell?
>
> He shoved the note into his pocket and hurried to class, glancing over his shoulder again and again.

This is a third-person point of view where we are still following a single character. You might also hear this referred to as a limited omniscient

voice because the narrator is the all-seeing author of the book, but the author chooses to follow one particular character instead of many different characters. It's very similar to first-person point of view, except now the narrator isn't telling you about something that happened directly to him, or even to someone he knows. He's telling you about someone else, and he has complete access to that person's thoughts, feelings, and past history.

In third person, the narrator often begins to fade from the page, and you become less concerned with who he is than who the characters are. Do you want your reader to be wondering about *you* halfway through your story about Jeff? Probably not. Instead, you hope to write with enough skill that the reader becomes completely enveloped in the world you've created. In third-person narration, the reader should be able to sit back and enjoy the ride, ready and able to suspend her disbelief in order to be taken on a wonderful journey.

This implicit contract between reader and narrator allows you as the writer to add multiple points of view if you wish. Since the narrator is the author, and the reader accepts that the author knows everything, there's no need to limit yourself to just one character's viewpoint. One common technique is to switch the focus back and forth between characters with each chapter. This can be done in first person as well. You could use two characters and go back and forth between their perspectives, as Rachel Cohn and David Levithan did in *Nick & Norah's Infinite Playlist*, or you could use a different character for each chapter throughout the novel as Ellen Wittlinger did in her novel *What's in a Name*. Using this type of narration can be a lot of fun when it's done well because it allows the reader to see the same events from multiple perspectives, and often each character adds his own unique twist to the plot.

THIRD-PERSON OMNISCIENT POINT OF VIEW

But what happens when there's no clear delineation between points of view? In the examples above, each chapter is still consistently focused throughout the narrative. What would happen if we wanted to shift between characters' points of view within a given page or paragraph?

Most of the time someone will mark the letters *POV* in the margin of your manuscript, meaning you should check to make sure you haven't made a mistake and your point of view remains consistent, but there is one occasion when you're allowed to jump back and forth between characters without any clear delineation between these sections. This is when you're using the omniscient point of view.

According to the *New Oxford American Dictionary*, the word *omniscient* means "knowing everything; having very extensive knowledge." If you get confused about what qualifies as the omniscient voice, go back to the meaning of the word. When you use the omniscient point of view, your narrator knows, well . . . *everything*. She can tell you what every character in the book is thinking and doing even when those characters are in separate places. Omniscient point of view has also been described as being "godlike" because the narrator sees all that's going on and can offer knowing commentary on events.

If I were using the omniscient point of view with the passage above, I could use the same text from version four, but I might tack on something like this afterwards:

> What Jeff didn't see was Charlie, hidden beneath the stairwell. Charlie who'd been watching him for weeks now, waiting for this exact moment. For Charlie, this day was far from his worst day ever—it was his best day, golden with potential.

> Charlie knew he should keep quiet, but he couldn't
> help it. He laughed out loud, then stopped and licked
> his lips. Revenge was sweet.

See how our perspective has expanded? Using the omniscient point of view we could expand it even further. How about adding this twist to the plot:

> Of course, neither one of them could have anticipated
> how trivial their argument was soon to become. Char-
> lie never would have expected to be out-villained by a
> girl, and Jeff, well Jeff would never know what hit him.

See how the narrator knows everything, even when the characters in question only have limited knowledge of what is happening? The omniscient narrator is not confined to one character's view point, therefore she can move easily between as many characters as necessary.

This is a very difficult point of view to use well. There's a reason we so seldom see the truly omniscient narrator in literature, and that's because the story can become muddled and the reader might fail to care about *any* of the characters when his allegiance is spread so thin. In the above example, who are you rooting for? Jeff? Charlie? The unnamed female? Obviously, this might become clearer as the backstory and plot are revealed, but the danger is that you won't end up rooting for anyone, and you'll find it easy to walk away from the book.

This is certainly not always the case. Robert Cormier used the third-person omniscient narrative voice beautifully in *The Chocolate War*, which I quoted earlier. Cormier uses it to add complexity and suspense to the story as each character's fate is drawn into question. The omniscient point of view can work well for suspense because the narrator can hint at trouble ahead that the characters themselves might still be unaware of.

Another book popular with teens that uses the omniscient point of view successfully is Douglas Adams's *The Hitchhiker's Guide to the Galaxy*. In this book the omniscient voice adds to the humor as the narrator jumps from the viewpoints of his characters—Arthur Dent, a muddled human being dragged into an adventure he wishes he wasn't having, Ford Prefect, an alien who was stranded on Earth for fifteen years posing as an out-of-work actor, and the various creatures they encounter, all of whom have strong opinions about Arthur, Ford, and earthlings in general. The omniscient point of view gives the author a perfect platform to comment on human behavior, and it adds to the humor of the book.

One final example of an author who uses the omniscient point of view is Paul Fleischman, who does so beautifully in his book *Breakout*. Fleischman adds his own unique twist by telling the story in chapters that alternate between a strict third-person narrative telling the story of teenage Del, a girl running away from her foster parents who gets stuck in a traffic jam as she's trying to escape, and a first-person omniscient narrator where a grown-up Del, also stuck in a traffic jam, imagines herself floating up out of her car, able to look into all the other cars and lives on the freeway.

It's important to note that even in a book as complex and varied as *Breakout*, the author is consistent within each section. When he writes in third person, the teenage Del must guess what other passengers stuck beside her are thinking. She knows only what those passengers tell her about their lives. When he writes in the first-person omniscient voice, he does not lapse into third-person narrative or suddenly switch narrators so we hear a different voice speaking to us.

Consistency is key when it comes to point of view. Decide whose eyes you are looking through, then stick with them.

SECOND-PERSON POINT OF VIEW

There's one last point of view we haven't discussed yet. Second-person point of view raises the question, "What if the eyes you're looking through are your own?" Not you as the storyteller, but you as the character? In second person, the reader is also the protagonist.

Here's how the passage we've been discussing would look rewritten into second person:

Version five:

> You walk down the hall, feeling good about the day. It's one of the first spring days and you've just found out you made the track team. You open your locker, reaching for your math book, and a note falls onto your sneaker. You pick it up. The paper is torn and crumpled as if someone had trouble fitting it through the slots.
>
> "What's this?" you wonder out loud.
>
> Then your blood runs cold.
>
> *I know all your secrets.*
>
> The words are scrawled across the page. Can they possibly mean what you think they mean? You look around wildly, but no one else is there. The hall is empty. Eerily silent.
>
> Your stomach turns and suddenly you know the truth. Life will never be the same again.

This type of narration has been used successfully in the suspense/thriller genre, and it works well for shorter passages, but it's difficult to sustain in part because of the repetition of the word "you," which has the same effect of calling someone by his name over and over again. It's also hard for the reader to suspend her disbelief since clearly she knows that she isn't the person you're describing and these events did not happen to her. As she reads your story, she might very well be thinking, "I would never do that!"

However, even second person can be used successfully. Author A.M. Jenkins used second-person point of view in her novel *Damage* about a high school football star suffering from depression. The use of second person echoes the emotional distance that the character is feeling and enables teens to relate to his mental state in a way they might not be able to if the author had chosen a different point of view.

Second person requires a lot of effort from your reader, and it demands even more work from you. If you decide to tackle this point of view, make sure you're ready to put in long hours making sure the words you use are good enough to overcome the barriers that second-person point of view puts in place between your reader and the suspension of disbelief. It can be accomplished to great effect, but choose wisely!

A Narrative Voice and Point of View Reading List

Want to further explore narrative voice and point of view? Try these books for unique narrative choices and interesting points of view:

- **1st Person Present Tense:** *Stuck in Neutral* by Terry Trueman—Shawn, the narrator of this book has cerebral

palsy. He has no muscle control and no way to communicate with his family, specifically his father who is considering "ending Shawn's pain" much to Shawn's dismay. This is a narrator with an exceptionally unique point of view.

- **1st Person Past Tense:** *Keturah and Lord Death* by Martine Leavitt—This book is a beautiful example of the range that narrative voices present in YA fiction. Keturah is a peasant girl who makes a bargain with death in order to find her true love. The stories she tells are full of rich, romantic language that is both precise and complex.

- **1st Person Omniscient:** *The Sledding Hill* by Chris Crutcher—When it comes to point of view, novels don't get much more complex than this one. Narrated by Billy, who is recently deceased, it tells the story of Eddie Proffit, a boy who has stopped talking after losing both his best friend (Billy) and his father. Now Billy, from beyond the grave, must find ways to help Eddie find his voice again.

- **2nd Person:** *Damage* by A.M. Jenkins—It's difficult to find good examples of second-person narration, but this book makes it work. A.M. Jenkins tells the story of Austin Reid, a football star who seems to have it all, but is actually dealing with depression. The author uses second person to create a distance that serves the story well.

Writing & Selling the *ya novel*

- **3rd Person:** *The Ropemaker* by Peter Dickinson—There are many, many examples of third person being used in YA fiction, but it's especially common to find this POV in fantasy and science fiction. Check out this award winning fantasy novel for one example of third person done well.

- **Omniscient:** *The Chocolate War* by Robert Cormier—This book is written by an exceptional writer, so it's a perfect way to learn by example. Study how Robert Cormier uses point of view to strengthen this unique story about a boy who refuses to participate in his school's fundraiser.

- **Multiple Narrative Voices or Points of View:** *Bronx Masquerade* by Nikki Grimes—In this novel, a teacher in the Bronx begins hosting an "open mike" day every Friday, thus allowing his students' voices to be heard. Each student is unique, so reading this book is a great way to study how one author can bring many different characters to life.

FINAL THOUGHTS ON NARRATIVE VOICE AND POINT OF VIEW

Choosing which point of view to use can be difficult, but it will always be necessary since every story uses narrative voice and point of view. No exceptions. If you're writing a novel, someone is telling

the story, even if that someone is you. Remember, the keys to using both effectively are:

- choices
- consistency
- finesse

Right from the start you must ask yourself what kind of story you're telling and what kind of tone you'd like to create. Do you want your narration to sound confessional? Contemporary? Then try first person, past or present tense. Is the setting an important part of the book, creating a strong mood that pervades the novel? Give third person a try. Do you need to portray broad, panoramic events that equally involve many characters? Experiment with the omniscient point of view.

Whichever choices you initially make, don't be afraid to abandon a point of view and start over using something else, even if you're far into the writing process. I once rewrote an entire novel from third person to first person after the first draft was complete! It was a time-consuming and tedious endeavor, but I had to make the choice that was best for my book. Sometimes what's best doesn't become clear until far into the process. When I was finished, I had a stronger book with a character who was more relatable than before.

No matter what, be consistent with the choices you make. Third person might have been the wrong choice for that novel, but I used it consistently throughout, and when I changed the book into first person, I was consistent with that, too. I didn't allow myself to write one section in third person and then slip into the character's own voice to tell about something else. Switching points of view breaks the spell of the novel, confusing the reader and drawing attention to the mechanics of writing.

Writing & Selling the *ya novel*

This brings us to finesse. Finesse is what a magician has that allows us to be mesmerized, taken in by every trick he performs. We don't see the mechanics of the trick, we see the illusion. Writers are magicians of the page. We use our words to create a world that the reader immerses herself in while she reads. Anything that detracts from this experience should be eliminated. You want your narrative voice to be strong, compelling, and *real*. This means that you not only shouldn't shift perspectives or move back and forth between past, present, and future tense without clear delineation, but you must also make your narrative voice as true to life as any voice the reader hears around him, while simultaneously maintaining the smooth flow of the text.

Challenging? Certainly, but it's a great challenge and I know you're ready. It's the kind of challenge that elevates good writing to great writing, entertainment to art. Narrative voice combines every aspect of what we've learned so far about characters, plot, and setting, plus it uses everything you'll learn next period in science class as we delve into the world of editing. It's a fundamental building block for every novel, and I guarantee the more you practice, the better you'll get at making the best choices and employing them with the most skill. So even though we're ready to move on to your next class, keep narrative voice in mind as we delve into the editing process.

Homework: Take this basic scenario and try writing one scene several different times, each time using a different point of view and/or a different narrative voice.

Plot: On her first day as a nursing home volunteer, a teen witnesses the death of an old man.

Focus on how you'd like your reader to feel. Use narrative voice to establish the teen's attitude and to establish distance or intimacy. Challenge yourself ... would there be a way to make this scene funny rather than serious? Which points of view work best for your various intentions?

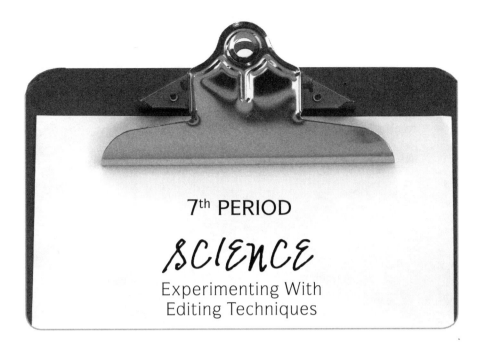

7th PERIOD

SCIENCE

Experimenting With
Editing Techniques

If science can, in part, be defined as "an expert's skillful technique" (according to the *New Oxford American Dictionary*), editing absolutely qualifies as a science. Many people think of editing merely as the correction of bad grammar, but in reality there's much more to it than that. Editing is not only about choosing or correcting individual words, it's also about looking at your work as a whole and deciding if the choices you made along the way are working as they should be. This can involve rewriting entire sections of a book or reordering events. Sometimes it means the elimination or addition of a character. Regardless, it's an opportunity to take your writing and make it better. Editing is something every author can be grateful for because it's a second chance to get things right. It can also be your third, fourth, and fifth chances as well.

It might be helpful to think of editing the way scientists think of the scientific method. When the first draft of a book is done, try to:

- observe your work impassively, doing your best to eliminate any emotional involvement that might make you defensive to change

- describe your own reactions

- predict how others might react

- exert control in order to eliminate alternatives that don't belong

- experiment to see which choices work best

- test your hypotheses about character, action, setting, and point of view. Do they really work the way you thought they would?

Most of us will need to experiment again and again in order to get things right. Just as scientists don't expect to prove a theory on their first try, very few writers know how their entire book should be written the first time through. It's necessary to see which paths work and which don't. This is nothing to be ashamed of. In fact, I think editing is something to be proud of. It shows you have the willingness and stamina to make your book the best it can be. So, if you're ready to get your hands dirty, let's get out those beakers and Bunsen burners and see what explodes.

WHEN TO BEGIN

I think the most daunting part of editing for many writers is the question of when to begin. Some writers start editing right away before they've even completed their first draft. Others are loath to edit at all, looking to send their work out as soon as that last word is typed. As with most things, a balanced approach is probably best.

Let's begin by looking at the dangers of editing too early. *What could be wrong with that?*, you might wonder. Isn't editing something we can always benefit from? On one level this is true. There are almost always changes that can be made to our writing, and nine times out of ten those changes will end up strengthening your novel. But what happens when you've turned your attention from the task of creating to the task of improving?

What's at stake is creative momentum. Momentum can be a powerful force to keep you moving through the writing process. Writing is not easy, and the task of finishing an entire book can be daunting, but it's easier to keep going when you're working hard and your story is flowing well than it is when you're picking something up cold. You know you've got momentum when each day's work leads into the next, and you just can't wait to finish the scene or chapter that you had to leave dangling the night before.

Think of momentum like going to the gym. For most of us, going to the gym takes some mental as well as physical effort. It can be hard to motivate yourself to get out of the house, especially if you've taken a long break for a vacation or illness. However, once you're working out, you remember why you wanted to exercise in the first place. Then it's easier to get to the gym again the next day. As long as you keep going, your momentum will remain high, but as soon as you stop … watch out!

Momentum is so important that I often write a small amount on both weekend days just to keep the story in my mind and to sustain the pattern of writing. As soon as I stop, I know it will be much harder to begin again. The first day back after a break I usually sit at my computer struggling to remember what it was I'd been so excited about the last time I wrote. This is why writers like Stephen King write every single day of the year. I'll admit, I'm not that diligent, but I do take momentum seriously, and when I have it I don't give it up easily.

Some authors deliberately end their day's work mid-scene just to keep their momentum rolling into the next day. By ending at the height of the action instead of wrapping up the scene or chapter, they're more anxious to finish what they started. Personally, I find that I need to complete my thoughts or else I don't remember them clearly the next day, but I can understand how for many people this technique works wonders.

Consider this: If momentum is so precious, why would you want to lose it too early in the process? You wouldn't. That's why editing too soon can be dangerous. When you stop the creative process in order to turn your attention to revising, the forward motion of the book stops. And for what? Unless your first draft is finished, it's probably too soon to see how the broader strokes of character and plot are working. You'll get to know your characters over time. Once you've lived with someone for two hundred pages, you'll know him a lot better than you would have at page fifty. And since your character's choices will affect the plot, allowing him to develop will allow the plot to unfold.

The most important accomplishment for your first draft of a novel is to finish it. Period. There will be plenty of time to fix things later, but in the beginning you want to move ahead and get your words down on the page. This is especially true if you haven't yet finished a complete manuscript. Many, many people start books and never end them. It's one of the reasons editors and agents want to see complete manuscripts rather than partials. You need to prove to them and to yourself that you have what it takes to see a book through to the finish line.

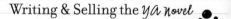

Now, having said all that, I will add a caveat. There is one way that editing and momentum can work together early on in the process. It may not work for everyone, but I've found that starting each day by rereading the chapter or section I was working on the day before is a great way to gather my thoughts for that new day, refreshing my memory and stoking the fire of creativity. As I read what I wrote, I edit lightly, changing awkward words or phrases, but I don't start too far back (no more than one chapter) and I don't spend too much time on the editing part of the task. My goal is to move forward, but if I can clean things up as I get ready to go, so much the better. If you're a disciplined person who won't get sidetracked, this approach might work for you. Otherwise, unless you've changed your mind about an important decision regarding character, plot, or setting—or unless you've discovered a glaring error that will affect the rest of your book—the time to edit is when your first draft is complete.

ONCE YOU FINISH YOUR FIRST DRAFT

Okay, so what happens once you've finished your first draft? Now the question moves from when to begin to *where* to begin. Should you start out on page one with your trusty red pen in hand? Should you hire a professional to help? Should you break out Strunk & White's *The Elements of Style* and search for editing tips?

If my most important piece of advice for this book can be summed up in one word—*read*—then my most important piece of advice for this chapter can also be summed up in one word: *wait*. If this seems contrary to the "learn-by-doing" approach of the rest of your school day, it's not. In this case, waiting *is* doing. It's a very important step in the editing process.

There's a term my editor and I throw around constantly: *fresh eyes*. What this refers to is the achievement of a certain amount of editorial distance from the work in question. When you're in the thick of writing or editing, reading passages again and again, this can be difficult to achieve, but it's necessary in order to view what you're working on as the reader would view it. Having fresh eyes means you're reading exactly what's on the page rather than what you intended to write. It means being able to sever some small part of the emotional attachment you might feel for your book in order to look at it objectively.

When I work with my editor, she and I both recognize the need for fresh eyes. We try to make sure that while the other person is working on the book, we don't look at it at all. In fact, I try not to even think about a novel until it's back in my hands. Why? Because I want my reading to replicate that of a first-time reader as closely as possible. I want to forget about what I know is going to happen next, or what I think I accomplished in terms of characterization. I want to distance myself from all the details of the world that have been dancing around in my imagination so I can see what I actually wrote. Making sure you've really communicated what you intended to communicate is a very important part of the writing process.

You'll be amazed at what you're able to see once you look at something from a distance. Maybe that character who was so real in your mind didn't make it completely on the page, and when you reread your work you'll realize which details you left out that are important for your audience. Maybe there are continuity errors in your plot. Perhaps your writing is wordy or sloppy. Maybe the novel doesn't flow the way you thought it would. You'll get a much better sense of your pacing and style after you've spent some time away from your work.

Spending time apart from your manuscript also gets you ready emotionally for accepting criticism. This is a tough part of the editing process, but it's also an essential part. No book is perfect the first time through. Have you heard the myth about Jack Kerouac's creation of *On the Road*? Legend says that Kerouac sat down at his typewriter, loaded up on coffee and Benzedrine, wrote the manuscript in one long scroll so he wouldn't have to stop to change sheets of paper in his typewriter, then sent it off to get published. You can still see the scroll today as part of an exhibit, but what most people don't realize is that it doesn't represent Kerouac's first draft. In fact, *On the Road* had already been done for years and had been rejected by every editor he'd sent it to. That famous scroll is actually a rewrite.

Why tell you this? I relate this story because Kerouac's *On the Road* has been used to give countless people permission to look at editing as something "beneath" truly gifted writers, but nothing could be farther from the truth. What makes a writer great is the work she produces, and whether that is the result of five drafts or fifty drafts doesn't matter. Accepting the fact that your first draft will be flawed will take the sting out of the critiquing that needs to happen in order for it to improve.

When you put your book away for a while, the heightened emotions that are necessary to drive you through the writing process have time to cool down, and you'll find you're able to read it almost as a different person. The amount of time to put away your work will vary, but two weeks is usually cited as a minimum. I aim for a month, if possible, with a first draft, but you'll want to find the time period that's right for you. Once you've sequestered your novel, be sure to mark the date to take it back out again. Fresh eyes are great, but abandoning your novel is *not* what you're looking to achieve.

WHAT'S YOUR BIGGEST PET PEEVE IN TEEN NOVELS? IS THERE ANYTHING AUTHORS DO THAT DRIVES YOU CRAZY?

Jessica, age 18, Washington: I hate novels that leave out huge plot lines. If you're writing a book about a high school senior, that person will be worrying about college, money, moving, graduation and friends. It's guaranteed. Many authors leave out huge things like this, and it drives me nuts!

April, age not given, New Mexico: My biggest pet peeve is that most authors don't have many positive things to say about teenagers. Usually they will write about the things teens do wrong, instead of positive things teens do.

Kathleen, age 17, New York: Stereotyping. I hate it when authors stereotype, even the antagonist. Also, it's not good when the author only shows one side of the story or the argument.

Maria, age 17, Michigan: My biggest pet peeve is that they use cheesy or outdated lines. If you want to know what the latest one-liner or cuss word is, don't go see the movie *Superbad*; go to a local movie theater and take notes on what the kids are saying in line or ask one in person.

McKenzie, age 14, Arizona: The one thing that teen authors often do that bugs me is milk a series. They will take a series that started out amazing and write too many books off the series to make more money. Don't ruin a good series!

Jessie, age 15, Maine: When they use stereotypes! Notice most teen novels have to do with sex and drugs.

Alicia, age 17, New Mexico: There's always some corny love story involved or the main character is either really popular and pretty or ugly and awkward. There's no kind of balance between the two.

Janis, age 16, New Jersey: That would definitely have to be references to old-time movie stars and old-time writers.

WATCHING FOR FLAWS

Now let's imagine that several weeks have passed. You take your manuscript out of the desk drawer where you put it and sit down, eager to read your amazing creation. You turn the pages, one by one, waiting to feel that same joy you felt when you were writing. Instead, your grin slowly fades and in place of the pride you'd been basking in (rightfully!) since finishing your book, you begin to feel a sickening kind of dread. The writing is sloppy. You can't tell who the main character is. The whole first section drags terribly. The location you thought you'd described so artfully now seems overdrawn. A quiet little voice starts to whisper in your ear, "This is the worst book ever written."

In the immortal words of Douglas Adams: "Don't panic!"

Banish that fear creeping up your spine that says your manuscript is unfixable. Silence the doubt that says you don't have the skill to improve your work. Editing, like anything else, is learnable, and the way to learn it is by diving in. You can do it, and if you're committed to being a published writer, you *will* do it. Remind yourself that professional writers edit their work many, many times both before and after they've handed it to an editor. Even if you're not published yet, if your goal is to be a professional author, you'll want to behave like one. Tell yourself that becoming your own best editor is just one more step in this process.

Here's what I look for on my first fresh read of my books. To begin with, I want to get a clear sense of the entire picture. Although it's tempting to tackle individual passages right away, I usually read the whole book from start to finish without changing anything so I can get a sense of how the plot plays out and how the pacing works. I make mental notes about dialogue that sounds stilted, sections that might need to get cut, or places where my main character gets lost in an array of too many conflicting people or themes. I'm trying to read the book as an independent reader might read it.

Once I've got an overview of the problem areas, I tackle the broader issues first. Since larger problems like characterization or plot development may require a lot of rewriting, I find that it saves time not to get too nitpicky about things like word choice and grammar at this stage. Entire passages are apt to be deleted or changed significantly.

Here's a list of some of the things you might watch for on your first pass of editing:

- How do you feel about the story? Do you still enjoy it? Do you have any trouble suspending your disbelief?

- Check your pacing. Are you turning the pages to see what happens next or is the text wordy and slow? Could the tension be taken up a notch or do events seem to occur organically, as if they couldn't happen in any other way?

- Watch for passages that seem self-indulgent. Samuel Johnson once said, "Read over your compositions, and when you meet a passage which you think is particularly fine, strike it out." While this might be a bit extreme, you do want to be aware of flowery passages that draw attention away from the story and to the writing itself.

- Keep an ear out for dialogue that sounds fake, and an eye out for long passages of uninterrupted text that might be changed into dialogue.

- See how you feel about your characters. Are you rooting for or despising the correct people? Do any of them get on your nerves? Do the secondary characters take over the book?

- How's the ending? Does the story seem to stop abruptly as if it suddenly plowed over a cliff? Or does it drag? Should it have ended several pages earlier?

- How's your beginning? Do you have a good opening line? Do you start with the action right away or does it take several pages before you begin the real story?

- Does information get passed along through the narrator telling the reader or through the reader seeing it for himself in active scenes?

- If you're writing humor, do you laugh in the right places? If you're writing horror, do you jump in the right places? If you're writing fantasy or science fiction, are the rules of your world consistent or do they shift throughout the book?

- Does your setting seem vivid, like a snapshot? Does it evoke the intended emotion?

- What can you strengthen to take the book from good to great?

No matter how you feel about your first draft, remember that you can take the time you need to get each element right. Many times, fixing one trouble spot will solve another one. For example, if your main character's motivation isn't clear and she's getting overshadowed by your secondary characters, that will affect your reader's ability to get drawn into the plot. Maybe part of the reason the main character doesn't come alive is because we never see her talking to anyone else and never get a sense of what she would say or how she'd interact with others. By adding more active scenes, suddenly her motivation becomes crystal clear. As the main character steps up to the plate, you'll find you're turning those pages with enthusiasm again.

In a good book, everything is woven together tightly and every change you make will affect the whole. Small changes can have big effects. Don't be fooled into thinking that every solution must be drastic. Large issues can sometimes hinge on single sentences.

BUT WHAT ABOUT THE "SMALL" STUFF?

You might be wondering … *When do we get to the grammar?* By focusing on broader issues am I implying you should ignore grammar and word choice and let a copy editor deal with that? Since you're writing a book for teens can you let it slide by? Absolutely not.

Although dialogue in YA novels might be less grammatical, it's still important that your book read well. And that is largely your responsibility. It's a common misconception that copyediting is where grammatical issues get fixed so the author doesn't need to worry about it on his own. Stories are told about writers who submitted their work with lots of mistakes and a brilliant agent or editor saw through their poor presentation, recognizing the literary gem underneath. These stories get rehashed again and again, so we feel okay about not completing a task that most of us find tedious. But the fact of the matter is, these stories are told because they are exceptions. Rare exceptions.

And they aren't exceptions because agents and editors lack vision. They are exceptions because sloppy presentation usually means laziness on the part of the author. Sure, we're not all grammar geniuses, but we can all learn the basics, and if we don't want to or can't, we can at least rope someone else into helping us clean up our text.

Your goal is to give your readers—whether they are editors, agents, friends, family, or strangers—the smoothest, most engaging read possible. You want them to be entertained or moved by what you've written, not annoyed at having to slog through a book that's cumbersome to read. Just as we only have one chance to make a first impression when we meet new people, our books only have one chance to make a first impression on readers. I highly recommend reading *The Elements of Style* if you haven't already. It's a small, thin book that's a classic reference tool. If the idea of reading a reference book (no matter how thin it is!) makes your hair stand on end, try either *Woe is I* by Patricia T. O'Conner or *Eats, Shoots & Leaves* by Lynne Truss. Both of these books make grammar entertaining.

Since it would be nearly impossible for me to give you a good grammatical overview in the course of one chapter, I'm going to focus my attention on the most important and most frequent line-editing issues I see in manuscripts. These can range from grammatical mistakes to word choices, but what they have in common is they are more detail oriented as opposed to the broader sweeping issues we covered above. I hope you'll apply for extra credit by furthering your grammatical studies after class.

Here are the line-editing problems I encounter most frequently in manuscripts:

Too many words. Manuscripts are often cluttered with needless words. Most of my early drafts are far too wordy, and if I read with an eye toward tightening my prose, I can take many of the excess words out. This not only streamlines the reading process, it makes every word count. Writing is not about putting as many words as possible onto a page; it's about choosing the very best ones.

Echoes. Echoes are words unnecessarily repeated in close proximity. An example would be these two sentences: "The phone rang insistently. Jack answered the phone and asked who was calling." *The phone* is an echo, so you'd want to come up with a creative way to reword your sentences. How about this instead: "The ringing of the telephone jolted Jack awake. He answered it gruffly. 'Who's calling?'" (Notice how the dialogue brings it alive?)

Too many sentences beginning with "And" and "But." Let's admit from the start that plenty of writers begin sentences with *And* or *But*. In moderation, I think this is okay, especially if it fits the narrative voice. BUT when used too often it can be very distracting. AND even if you have a good reason, if you find yourself using these words as sentence starters too often, try something else.

Writing & Selling the *ya novel*

Using punctuation in place of plot. We won't get into rules for submitting your manuscript until the next chapter, but I can tell you one thing right now: One of the surest signs that a manuscript is weak is the overuse of the exclamation point. What's wrong with the exclamation point? If a reader sees it too often it begins to have a numbing effect, and chances are the author is using it to convey excitement that ought to be found within the text. Make your plot exciting, not your punctuation. This applies to overuse of the dash, ellipsis, semicolon, bold, and italics as well. If it's out of the ordinary, use it sparingly. Save attention-grabbers for the times when you most need them.

Repeating information. Many beginning writers lack confidence that they're getting their point across so they repeat information many times throughout the text. Maybe it's a scene in which a character rehashes what happened earlier in the novel, or perhaps it's the narrator reminding us of what we already know. Either way, make sure information isn't repeated unnecessarily. Trust your reader to have gotten it the first time. Teens are a sharp, intelligent audience.

Too many adjectives. This is a variation on the same theme. One form that not trusting your reader can take is cluttering the text with too many adjectives. We don't think that one descriptive word will do the trick, so we throw in a synonym. Or maybe we don't trust our readers to imagine the scene exactly as it is in our heads, so we keep describing and describing and describing. But the reality is, readers are never going to see something in the exact same way we see it, so we need to choose the best, most important words to get our point across. Then we need to let go and allow the reader's imagination to take control of the story.

Overuse of names in dialogue. This is a pet peeve of mine, and I almost hate to mention it because once you notice it, you can't *stop* noticing it. Pay close attention to how often you use someone's name in the course of a real-life conversation. Then watch how often people in books use each other's names. You'll find that characters call other characters by their names constantly, often referring to them by name several times in the course of the same conversation. Now look at an early draft of your manuscript. If you're like most people, you'll find this same discrepancy. Unfortunately, this tendency can grate on the nerves and ruins the realism and rhythm of dialogue.

Lack of verbs. When you read through your text, pay special attention to sentence fragments. Not only are they grammatically incorrect, but sentence fragments tend to leave out verbs. Verbs are how we convey action, and as you know, action is the foundation of both plot and characterization. Sometimes sentence fragments can be used for great effect, but beware of using them too often, leaving your manuscript verb-depleted.

Poor spelling. Have you ever received an e-mail that was so full of spelling errors and abbreviations you could barely read it? While spelling does not need to be perfect when you submit your work, it does need to be passable. Remember to use spell-check. While other people in your life may or may not notice spelling errors, it's an editor's job to notice. One or two spelling errors aren't cause for rejection, but multiple errors on each page might be enough to tip the scales in favor of someone else's manuscript.

FINDING FABULOUS FIRST READERS

So now you've cleaned up your text and you're ready to submit it to editors, right? You've completed a first draft, put the manuscript away, and rewritten it in order to strengthen your plot. You've tested your original story hypothesis until you're sure no one can argue with your results. Can I really tell you to do more before sending out your work? Unfortunately, I must.

There's one last very important step in the scientific method that should be mirrored in the writing process. *Replication of results.* When a scientist does an experiment and comes up with a conclusion, the result is not considered valid unless it can be replicated. The same can be said for getting published. Although you might think your manuscript is ready to be on a bookstore shelf, it won't ever get published unless someone else agrees. At the most basic level, at least one other person—an editor—needs to agree with your opinion of your work. More realistically, the entire editorial board at a publishing house must agree, and then hopefully, readers will also agree. Without this outside verification, your work will not fit into the boundaries of traditional publishing.

Making the editors and agents you're submitting to your first readers is a foolish way to find out if you can replicate your results. Why not test your book with other readers first? That way, should these readers suggest changes you agree with, or should you hear the same feedback over and over again, you can consider making alterations before submitting your work for publication.

But how do you find the right readers? Should you give your novel to teens or adults? Should you pay someone to critique your work? How many people should you ask? These are important questions. By now you've worked long and hard on your book, so you want to give it a fair shot. You want honest, informed, critical feedback. This might rule out your mom. (Unless, of course, your mom happens to be a librarian who's well versed in teen novels, like mine!)

What you want to avoid is giving your book to someone who would never in a million years pick it up off a bookshelf. You also want to avoid giving it to someone who will tell you only what you want to hear. Or worse yet, someone who can't articulate her thoughts. There's nothing more disappointing than waiting weeks to get a reader's response and then hearing, "I liked it." Of course you're glad he liked it, but this offers you nothing in terms of constructive criticism.

You want to find readers who read YA books, who you think will be able to articulate their reactions clearly, and who you can stand to hear brutally honest feedback from. Teachers and librarians make excellent readers. Teenagers can be fabulous readers if you choose teens who love to read and are good at expressing themselves. Other writers make wonderful readers, too; that's why so many authors join writers' groups. Writers know exactly what to watch out for because they're going through the same process with their own work.

Successful writers' groups come in many forms. They can involve any number of people and can meet in person or communicate via e-mail or snail mail. The only thing that's essential to finding the right writers' group is that you can give and receive meaningful feedback with the other writers involved. To find a writers' group in your area, check with the Society of Children's Book Writers & Illustrators (SCBWI) if you're a member, visit your local library or bookstore, post a query on an online forum, or attend a writers conference or workshop and ask people you meet there. If you have no luck finding an established group to join, don't be afraid to start your own! There might be someone else, just like you, hoping to connect with other writers, and if you post a sign or place an ad you might be surprised at the response.

Remember, even if you find the very best readers possible, writing is still a subjective activity. Be sure to weigh the thoughts and opinions of multiple readers before making drastic changes. Hearing from as many readers as possible, and being aware of each reader's strengths and weaknesses, will allow you to put the feedback you receive into perspective.

Don't be afraid to ask your readers questions as well. Instead of passively accepting that they felt a certain way, try to find our *why* they felt that way. Sometimes, it's not the cited problem that needs to be changed but something else that is an *underlying* problem. You might even consider using the editing lists found in this chapter as guidelines to asking your readers key questions. They might not offer certain information on their own, but with a little help they might be able to tell you exactly where your book's pacing slowed or your plot seemed unbelievable.

Why Participate in a Writers' Group?

- You'll gain knowledgeable readers for your work.
- You'll learn from others as you read their writing.
- Critiquing your fellow writers can help you to take critique from agents and editors. You'll know how it feels to be on both sides of the equation.
- Meeting with a group can keep you on track, forcing you to produce on schedule.
- Your writers' group can encourage you when you're discouraged.
- You can share information about editors and agents. Other writers can help you find out who's looking for YA material and what kind of respopnse time you might experience when you send out your manuscript or query letters.

- It's fun! Potluck? Wine and cheese? Desserts only? Movie afterwards? Be creative and have a good time.

Tips for Making Writers' Groups Work

- Make sure your feedback is balanced. Don't read other people's work looking only for mistakes.
- Be a good listener. Don't interrupt or try to explain your intentions.
- Don't be defensive! If you think someone's criticism is off track, say, "I'll consider that." Then think about it later when you're calm.
- Give praise first, critique second.
- Don't let one person dominate the discussion.
- Take turns sharing; try making up a schedule ahead of time to avoid conflict later on.
- Don't let jealousy sabotage your relationships. Applaud each other's successes; if you keep working, your time will come.
- Don't be afraid to bow out if a group simply is not working for you.

OTHER SOURCES OF EDITING HELP

Finding the right readers is a lot harder than it seems. Trust me. I've learned the hard way. The first reader I ever gave one of my novels to (it was a fantasy novel) was an English professor who started out his feedback by saying, "I've always hated fantasy. One of my best friends wrote a fantasy novel and I've never been able to bring myself to read it."

One of the first readers of *Fat Kid Rules the World* suggested that my novel would be better off if the main character lost weight and became the prom king—something totally antithetical to the theme of the book. Yet another early reader unexpectedly joined the Army, taking the only printed copy of my book with him. I never heard from him again.

There are times when finding a professional might be your best approach. Finding a professional reader does not mean sending your manuscript to an agent or editor who charges reading fees. Those people are very *un*professional. Agents and editors make their money off the sale of your book, either through commission when they sell it to a publishing house or through their salary and bonuses if they're the ones publishing it. If they're charging reading fees, they're probably not on the up-and-up.

So how do you find a professional? For most people this means attending a conference or workshop, or taking a class. Classes are available not only through universities, but online as well. You'll find that taking a class is one of the best ways to improve your skills, energize your writing, and meet other people who love to do the same thing you love to do. Many writers' groups form as extensions of class settings. Workshops and conferences are also great ways to meet people and learn about your craft. A lot of conferences offer professional critiques on a limited number of pages as part of your registration fee. Professional organizations like SCBWI not only host their own conferences but can keep you abreast of activities happening in your area.

Another source of professional help might be finding a book doctor. I'll be completely honest here; even though I offer a manuscript critique service, I wouldn't recommend this for everyone. Make sure you're really ready to hear detailed feedback if you decide to submit your manuscript. There are times when I suspect someone might have been hoping for a completely glowing response from me, but that's not why you pay someone to read your work. There are plenty of friends and family who can offer that.

If you decide to use a book doctor, make sure you've done everything you know how to do before you submit your work. Not because you need to impress that person, but because you want to get your money's worth! Why pay someone to tell you something you could have figured out on your own? What you're looking for from a professional manuscript critique is insight that can't be gained without that person's professional expertise. I also advise you to get a recommendation whenever possible.

One source of recommendations is SCBWI's *Freelance Editors & Manuscript Doctors* list that's available to SCBWI members. Another source is online chat rooms where writers discuss who they've worked with and whether they were happy with the services they received. You'll find ads for freelance editors in the back of most writing magazines, but I'd definitely advise you to ask around before blindly following an advertisement. If you do choose to call someone you don't know, ask her if she has references you might call or e-mail, and make sure she's open to reading teen fiction

FINAL ADVICE

No matter how you approach the editing process, making your book as strong as it can be is your ultimate goal. Why? Because teens are critical, discerning readers and they deserve our very best. Just as scientists set rigorous standards so they can add knowledge to the world, writers set rigorous standards so we can add literature to the world. We want our books to edify, entertain, and illuminate the teens who read them. Editing is our chance to take our raw words and refine them into gold.

Homework:

It's time to invest in your writing. Choose one extra-curricular activity to pursue: find a writers' group, sign up for a one-day workshop, read a grammar book, join SCBWI, register for a class, book yourself a conference. No excuses!

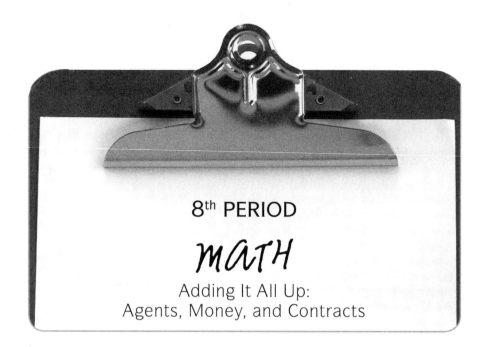

8th PERIOD

MATH

Adding It All Up:
Agents, Money, and Contracts

Even if math was never your favorite subject, it's a topic that writers ignore at their own peril. Sure, it would be nice if we could operate wholly on the level of story choices, focusing on achieving our desired degree of literary merit, but at the end of the day, if you want to write for a living, you need to think about money as well.

When it comes to money, there's good news and bad news. The good news is you *can* make money as a writer. The bad news is that very, very few of us will ever achieve best-seller status, so it isn't always easy. Still, many writers are able to bring in steady incomes, or at least partial incomes based on their work. Remember that even if your sole desire is to produce great literature, that involves reaching your audience, and part of reaching your audience means getting compensation for your work and making sure your book gets distributed to the teens who will read it.

Let's turn our attention to the steps you need to take to go from unpublished writer to published author. Making this move requires that you decide exactly what kind of publication you want to pursue, so we'll start by examining the various marketplaces for your work. If you choose traditional publishing as your best venue, you'll also want to delve into the questions of submitting to agents vs. editors, preparing your manuscript and query letters, and negotiating a solid contract if you decide to submit your work without an agent.

PATHS TO PUBLICATION

SELF-PUBLISHING

Many authors perceive publication by a major publishing house as the one and only pathway to publishing their book, but this is not the case. Self-publishing used to be too expensive for the average person to afford, and the end product did not always have a professional look. Once you got your bound book it was very difficult to market it and actually sell copies.

This is beginning to change.

These days, self-publishing is within most people's budgets. A quick search on the Internet revealed prices as low as 199 dollars, though costs can be much, much more depending on whether you choose to hire your own editor, copy editor, illustrator, or book designer, and whether you choose a company that will take care of printing and distribution or you decide to coordinate production and distribution yourself. Either way, you can definitely end up with a professional-looking product with cover art that's virtually indistinguishable from the books you'd find in Barnes & Noble.

When it comes to marketing your book, self-publishing companies sometimes offer free Web sites as part of their publishing package, and even if they don't, most of us can find someone to create a Web site for us at a reasonable price or we can make our own. Books can also be sold through the online versions of most of the major chain stores, through advertisements, directly to independent booksellers, and via fax, e-mail, or telephone, just to name a few options. This variety makes them accessible to audiences in a whole new way. As self-publishing becomes more common and more commercial, it's losing its stigma and more people are viewing it as a viable option, not just a last resort.

So why choose to self-publish? Self-publishing can allow you to get your book out to your audience even if you don't find success in the traditional marketplace. It can offer reward for all your hard work as you see your words in print for the first time. Increasingly, authors are also turning to self-publishing to keep a higher degree of control in the publishing process. Working under contract with a publishing house demands a lot of compromise, and many times you have no leeway to fight things that might seem unfair. For example, I might think that devoting a huge slice of a publishing house's marketing budget to Madonna, who is already a superstar and does not need the publicity, and whose books received overwhelmingly bad reviews, is unfair to writers who are working hard to turn out quality literature in their chosen field. (Just an example ... hypothetically, of course.) But as one author on a publisher's list I have no say in where they invest their money. Some people would rather handle the publication, cover design, and distribution of their books on their own with no one else to answer to in terms of content or marketing decisions. Self-publishing can also

0123456789   +   ÷   ▬

offer more security since publishing houses tend to be bought and sold, and editors move from house to house frequently, abandoning books and stalling the careers of aspiring authors.

If you do decide to self-publish, I would warn you about a few things. First, do your research. As with anything, you want to make sure the company you choose is reputable. If you choose to handle the printing and distribution yourself, you want to be sure you really have the time, energy, and resources to handle this task. If you don't know anyone who has self-published his work, ask your local bookstore owner if she does, or join one of the many online chat rooms where authors converse on forums about every topic under the sun. Forums might seem intimidating if you've never posted on one before, but they're a great way to gather anecdotal information. You should also look for books on the subject such as *The Complete Guide to Self-Publishing* by Tom and Marilyn Ross or *Dan Pointer's Self-Publishing Manual*.

Second, since you're trying to reach teenagers, you must take into consideration the fact that a huge percentage of YA sales come from schools and libraries that usually buy their books from traditional publishing sources. They often make their choices about what to buy based on major review publications such as *Booklist*, *The Horn Book*, and *Kirkus Reviews*, and these publications may not be receptive to self-published books. Since there are so many titles competing for review attention and for bookshelf space, you'll have a difficult time breaking into these important teen markets if you self-publish. Ask yourself if you'll really be able to reach the number of teens you desire using your own marketing plan. Do you have the time and the personal connections to coordinate school and library visits to sell your book? Will a Web site be enough to convince a teenager to take a chance on buying your book?

Finally, the paths of traditional publishing and self-publishing do not mix very well. Many people mistakenly see self-publishing as an "in" with agents and editors. Their logic is that once the agent or editor sees their manuscript as a real book, typeset and bound, it will be that much easier to see its potential. If you could pay 199 dollars to guarantee your book would be taken seriously in a competitive situation, wouldn't you do it?

Unfortunately, it doesn't really work this way. Agents and editors know their jobs very well, and what they're interested in is content. No amount of clever packaging is going to make them buy your book if it isn't what they're looking for. If anything, self-publishing can work against you. Although the stigma against self-publication is diminishing in the marketplace, it's still occasionally present in the slush pile. You don't want an editor or agent's first thought upon picking up your book to be: "I bet this made the submission rounds already and got rejected by everyone and that's why the author self-published it."

Many agencies and publishing houses have very strict guidelines for submissions of manuscripts, and these are almost always unbound, Times New Roman 12-point font, double-spaced, black ink on white paper. By submitting something in a different format, you're not only failing to gain an advantage; you might be giving someone a reason to return your book unread.

If an agent or editor does read your self-published book and likes it, you'll have questions to answer that you wouldn't have had to answer otherwise. During my time at Curtis Brown, Ltd., we sold one self-published book, in part due to the fact that the author had obtained an advance quote from a best-selling author, and in part because he'd had phenomenal success selling the book through local stores. Of course, it was also a fabulous story. However, the question of sales figures was an issue right from the beginning. Publishers wanted to know how many copies he'd already sold, and there was a fine line between impressing them with numbers large enough but not scaring them away by having cut down on *their* potential sales by already reaching too large a percentage of the audience. Generally speaking, publishers want to start fresh.

Remember, self-publishing is not an "in" to traditional publishing. It *is* an alternative pathway for your books to meet an audience. If you feel certain that your book is ready to be published, but you can't find the right publishing house, or if you just feel like you could do a better job publishing it on your own, it's an increasingly accessible option that more and more authors are making work for them. Just be sure you have a solid marketing plan so your freshly bound book can find its way into the hands of teen readers.

SMALLER PUBLISHING HOUSES

In between the option of self-publishing and selling your book to a major publishing house, there's another option that many people overlook. This is selling your work to a smaller, independent publishing house. Small presses generally publish fewer titles per year and have smaller print runs than larger publishing houses. The terms "small" and "independent" are often used interchangeably, but independent actually refers to the fact that a publishing house is not part of a conglomerate.

There are many such small and independent publishing houses available once you start looking. In fact, according to the Small Press Center (www.smallpress.org) there are an estimated seventy thousand! They range from very tiny houses that might only publish a couple titles a year to renowned publishing houses that, although they have limited lists, are quite well known.

But how many of those presses publish books for teens? Good question. Writing YA definitely cuts down on the number of small publishing houses that will be interested in publishing your book; however, according to SCBWI's *Small Press Markets Guide*, there were over seventy small presses that responded positively when asked if they'd be open to receiving unsolicited submissions from SCBWI members. Of those, many publish books for teens. If you'd like to access this list you can find it at www.scbwi.org, but you'll need to be an SCBWI member first. If you're not an SCBWI member you can use the Internet to find the guidelines and descriptions for most small presses.

Whether you're reviewing a list such as the one provided by SCBWI or doing your own research, you'll notice that many smaller houses are niche publishers. They may focus on one type of material or subject matter, so they're able to do a very thorough job of covering a chosen field—often filling gaps in traditional publishing lists. Examples might include houses that exclusively publish Christian books; exclusively gay, lesbian, bisexual and transgender-related titles; or books that take place in a certain geographical area, such as Southwestern books, or titles that take place in New England. You'll also find many nonprofit small presses that publish political books. Although admittedly it's harder to find teen categories within these niches, they do exist and sometimes can be exactly the right home for your novel.

One of the biggest advantages to being published by a small press is finding a place for a book that falls outside traditional publishing boundaries. Perhaps your manuscript keeps getting rejected and you suspect it's because your work tackles a subject that falls between the cracks in larger publishing houses. Turning your attention to smaller presses might allow you to find your perfect match—a publisher that not only appreciates your work but also knows who to market it to. Their print run might be smaller, but they might be able to get your book into the hands of the exact teens who will most love to read it.

PRINT-ON-DEMAND AND E-BOOKS

It's worth mentioning both print-on-demand publishing and e-books, although these fields are rapidly changing, and at the present time I wouldn't recommend either as a path to self-publication. Print-on-demand is a type of technology where single copies of a book are printed as orders are received rather than producing an entire print run. E-books are the electronic versions of books, downloaded to and read from portable electronic reading devices. Both of these publishing venues are discussed often, sometimes being touted as the future of publishing, but both still have serious drawbacks.

Print-on-demand books tend to have higher cover prices, making them more difficult to sell, but more disturbingly, authors don't always control the rights to their books. Instead, they receive a royalty on each book sold while the publisher holds exclusive or nonexclusive rights to their titles. This is something to be aware of. If you are *self*-publishing, then *you* should control the rights to your book. No exceptions.

E-books present a different type of rights issue. This time, it might not be the publisher infringing on your rights, it might be your customers. As of now, e-books can easily be copied and/or illegally downloaded, cutting down on your profits. They also require expensive reading devices that prohibit many potential readers from accessing them. Most teens probably don't own an e-book reader and are unlikely to spend the money on one just to download your book.

Again, both of these fields are changing quickly, so who knows what the future will hold. One thing that can be said for teenagers is they're often way ahead of adults when it comes to accessing technology and embracing change. Even now I'm sure you will find success stories in both markets. For those of you willing to put in the extra time and research needed to explore fields in flux, you might find yourself on the forefront of innovation.

TRADITIONAL PUBLISHING

For the vast majority of us, despite the many other options available, traditional publishing will still be the path we choose. Why? This is math class, so let's consider this word problem: If a small press prints one thousand copies of your book and distributes them to X stores, and a large press prints five thousand copies of the first run of your book and distributes them to Y stores, then goes back to press and prints five thousand more, who will make more money if the book is priced the same in both cases, the author publishing with the small press or the large press? Assuming Y is greater than X, the answer seems obvious. The person publishing with the larger publishing house will make more money. In actuality, the amount of money an author makes can depend on what type of advance the author received from either house, what kind of royalties she's making, and whether there are any returns of the books sold, but for now, let's set those issues aside and focus on the advantages to traditional publishing.

The reason so many people choose larger publishing houses is because they can allow your books to reach the largest possible audience.

This, in turn, can lead to the greatest amount of profit from your work. Traditional publishing houses have large distribution networks, professional book designers who know what attracts teen readers, and marketing teams who will help your book reach teens everywhere it possibly can.

So how does one enter this world? I'll tell you right now, it isn't easy, but it isn't impossible, either. And if you're able to sell your book, the rewards can be great. Let's turn our attention to the submission process and see how you can get your manuscript into the hands of as many teens as possible.

Teen Panel

WOULD YOU READ (OR HAVE YOU READ) AN ELECTRONIC BOOK (E-BOOK)? WHY OR WHY NOT?

(Author's Note: The vast majority of the teens surveyed had either never heard of an electronic book or had a misconception of what an e-book actually was. Of those who were familiar with the term, most kids did not think they'd want to read one or had read one and didn't like it. Only twenty kids out of the ninety surveyed said they'd consider reading an e-book.)

Erin, age 16, Idaho: I read an e-book once, but didn't enjoy it. There's something about having a book in your hands, flipping through the pages and breathing in its wonderful scent; hugging it to yourself in a good spot, or clutching it for dear life in an intense part. You don't get that experience with a digital book.

Kymmie, age 13, New York: I have never heard of e-books until now! That sounds cool. I'll read one and see!

Rita, age 16, New Mexico: Yes, I would read an electronic book because it sounds interesting.

Alicia, age 17, Michigan: No, I have not read a whole one. I tried, but I need the physical holding of the book so I can lay down and read and be comfortable.

Emily, age 17, Michigan: I would read an e-book because it is better for the environment and it is a new experience.

Devin, age 16, New Mexico: No, I've never done that. I'm too poor for that.

McKenzie, age 14, Arizona: No, I have not read an e-book and do not plan to in the future because books were not meant to be read electronically. I like them the old-fashioned way. Always have and always will.

SUBMITTING YOUR WORK

AGENTS VS. EDITORS

The question of whether to use an agent or submit directly to editors is one you will hear constantly discussed among writers. Since I used to work at a literary agency, one might say I'm biased when it comes to this subject. But you could also say I have the inside scoop! How many jobs have you worked at where you came away feeling as if you would never again use their particular product? It's common to hear people say things like, "After working at that fast-food place, I will never again eat fast food." or "Since working for that computer company, I always buy from their competition." My experience has been the opposite.

Both as a former employee and as a writer who still uses their services, I absolutely recommend getting an agent if you can. What does an agent do? A literary agent acts as the middleman between authors and editors. He sends your work to publishing houses, and if it sells he negotiates your contract and takes a commission—usually 15 percent—of your earnings.

The reason some people prefer to bypass agents and submit to editors directly is twofold. First, it takes just as much time and effort to find an agent as it does to find an editor, and as with any field, you're not guaranteed to find a good one. Many people prefer to handle things on their own rather than risk ending up with an agent they're not well matched with. They can speed up the submission process by sending their material directly to the editors who can acquire it for the publishing house without having to wait for an agent to send out their work. They'd also rather not pay commission on the sale of their work. Agents receive commission on your royalties as well, so that can add up to a lot of money if your books are good sellers. Some writers feel that with a little ingenuity or a friend who's a lawyer, a writer can negotiate her own contract and save herself money in the long run.

Here are the flip sides to those arguments.

Yes, it does take a lot of work to find an agent, but once you've found one you're compatible with she can be well worth the effort. An agent spends a good portion of her time networking with editors.

They meet at conferences, have lunch together, and correspond regularly regarding established clients. An agent knows which editors are looking for different types of material, whose plate is empty and who is swamped with submissions, who has a fondness for cats and probably can't resist your story about the teen who rescues kittens from city streets, and who can't stand fantasy so if you send her your boy wizard novel it's a guaranteed rejection. Since agents have personal and business relationships with editors, your manuscript is more likely to get read and more likely to be read in a timely manner. Many publishing houses state outright that they won't accept unagented submissions.

In case this policy sounds unnecessarily harsh, I can testify to the incredible volume of material that is submitted every week to agents and editors. It's daunting to see how many people are fighting for so few publishing slots. By only accepting agented work, publishing houses are cutting down on the number of submissions and hopefully insuring a certain level of quality. This is another advantage to having an agent. Agented manuscripts arrive with a stamp of approval. Remember the final step in the scientific method we learned about in science class—replication of results? Well, when an editor sees a manuscript that's submitted by an agent, he already knows that at least one person (and probably several) liked this book enough to choose it above the rest of the pack.

I don't want to overstate my case, though. A common misconception among aspiring authors is that finding an agent means a guaranteed sale to a publishing house. When I first started working at Curtis Brown, Ltd. I had this same idea, but I quickly learned otherwise. The material that agents submit is rejected frequently. Just because an agent thinks it will sell doesn't mean it will. The market changes all the time and what strikes one person as fantastic can fail to find a fan in someone else.

But let's say your novel does sell. Agents can negotiate better contracts than the vast majority of us could on our own. They can usually get you a higher advance right up front. There are two reasons for this. First, since they're trained to negotiate contracts and they do it regularly, they know what to ask for. They know what other authors have received and what different publishing houses offer. This leads to the second part of the equation: They're not afraid to ask for what they know they can get.

Here's another word problem for you: If an editor makes an offer for 10,000 dollars on a first novel and the writer is ready to agree to this offer, but the agent says, "No, let's ask for 12,500 dollars," how much commission did the agent earn if she were charging the industry standard of 15 percent? Less the agent's commission, how much more money did the author make than he would have made if he'd accepted the original offer?

Answer: The agent earned 1,875 dollars. The difference between the original offer and what the agent earned is 2,500 dollars. Thus the author made 625 dollars more than he would have, even *after* he paid the agent's commission.

Now let's tackle a second word problem: If an agent negotiates a hardcover royalty that starts at 10 percent instead of the 8 percent that was originally offered, and your book earns 100,000 dollars over the next few years, how much more money did you make off that higher royalty after the agent's commission is subtracted?

Answer: Ten percent of 100,000 dollars is 10,000 dollars. Eight percent is 8,000 dollars. So you made 2,000 dollars more than you would have made with the lower royalty. At 15 percent, the agent's commission from 10,000 dollars would be 1,500 dollars. So you made 500 dollars *more than you would have*, even after you paid the agent's commission.

Can you begin to see how these numbers might stack up? Good agents should be able to negotiate back their fees and then some. They end up costing you nothing. And even if you do eventually pay them out of your profitable sales, the service they offer is an important one that's worth the money. Agents make sure your contract doesn't rope you into something you might later regret, and they will act as your advocate if you hit a bump in the publishing process, such as a disagreement with an editor, cover art you hate, or a change of publishing houses mid-career. Publishing doesn't always go smoothly, and when things go wrong it's nice to have someone on your side so you don't have to muddy the editorial waters by arguing on your own behalf.

TARGETING YOUR SUBMISSIONS

Regardless of whether you decide to submit to editors directly or find an agent first, you still need to know how to submit your work. Manuscript submission is a long and sometimes arduous process, so you will do well to learn all you can before you begin. You only get one shot to submit your book to an agent or editor, so you'll want to use that opportunity wisely.

Let's start with deciding who to submit to. Presumably you've narrowed your choices to agents or editors. If you're looking for agents I highly recommend submitting to agents listed in the Association of Authors' Representatives (AAR) directory found at www.aar-online. org. The AAR holds its members to professional and ethical standards so you're far less apt to find a rotten apple.

You can search for both editors and agents through resources such as SCBWI's *Market Survey of Publishers of Books for Young People*, their *Small Press Markets Guide*, and their *Agents Directory* (all of these publications are for members only); *Children's Writer's & Illustrator's Market*, which includes information specifically for the children's and YA market; or *Jeff Herman's Guide to Book Publishers, Editors & Literary Agents*, which offers information on all types of publishers and agents. You'll find these publications are the staples every writer needs to navigate the submission waters. Not only do they include editors' and agents' contact information, but they usually give a brief description of what type of material the editor or agent prefers along with guidelines for submission. Read through these guidelines so you know which editors accept unagented material, which publishing houses won't accept e-mail submissions (few do), and which houses won't accept multiple submissions. You'll want to pay particular attention to which editors and agents handle teen fiction. This will save you a lot of time, energy, and postage.

Here's another word problem to illustrate my point: If an author sends out ten query letters, and each large-size mailing envelope cost nineteen cents and the postage cost sixty-seven cents, and within each envelope there is also a self-addressed return envelope that cost ten cents with another stamp on it that cost forty-one cents, how much did the author spend on all ten submissions, not including paper, printing costs, and gas for his car?

Answer: $13.70

This may not seem like a lot, but you will probably send out far more than ten query letters over the course of the submission process. It makes much more sense to target your queries to individuals who are interested in the type of work you're submitting than to blanket the field with submissions that will only get returned.

QUERY LETTERS

Right about now, you might be thinking, "What is a query letter anyway?" Important question. Here's your answer:

A query letter is a letter sent to an agent or editor asking if she'd be interested in reading your manuscript. Query letters are generally limited to one page, and they are a standard business letter telling the person you're addressing a little bit about your book, your credentials as a writer, and anything else you think is appropriate to include. Query letters are your way of introducing yourself and your YA novel to agents and editors—and we all know how important first impressions are.

A large part of my job at Curtis Brown, Ltd., included reading query letters, so I can definitely give you some pointers as to what works well and what does not. Let's start with the positive:

- Be professional.

- Keep your letter brief.

- Pay attention to presentation, making sure your query is clean, well written, and printed on good paper.

- Make your first line matter.

- Follow the rules. If an agent or editor requests a self-addressed stamped envelope (SASE), make sure you include one.

- Include every writing credential you can claim. If you wrote for your college newspaper, mention your numerous published articles.

- Mention any connections you might have with the person you're sending the letter to. If you met him at a conference, or if you have a mutual acquaintance, put that in your opening sentence.

- Reference other YA books the editor or agent handles if they're among your favorites. This is a nice way to personalize your letter, showing you've done your research and have common tastes and interests with the person you're submitting to. (Helpful hint: To find out who represents your favorite authors, check the acknowledgments in their books to see if the author has thanked her editor or agent. If you're an SCBWI member, look for their publication called *Edited By: A House-by-House Listing of Editorial Credits.*)

- Mention if you are submitting to more than one agent or editor simultaneously.

- Take time to make sure your letter is as perfect as it can be.

Here are some things you should NOT do:

- Don't reference your parents, your children, your grandparents, or your students (if you're a teacher) as the reason you believe your work will sell. Everyone has people who love them and will support their work no matter what, and even though you might know that your teenage daughter is a tough critic, putting this in your query letter won't help sell your book.

- Don't try to be gimmicky. Yes, you do need to grab an agent or editor's attention, but you should do this by making sure your letter is well written and makes your book sound irresistible.

- Don't pitch a book you haven't finished writing yet. Not only is a timely submission important should an agent or editor request your work, but you want to leave plenty of time to edit. Rushing through a first draft in order to fulfill a request probably means you've blown your chance to impress someone who liked your premise.

- Don't try to sell two books at once. Query letters are limited in space, so you want to use every word wisely. It's very rare for an editor or agent to take on two books by a new author at the same time, even if you present them as a series. Pitching two books at once makes *you* your own competition. It's also likely that if one book sounds like a possible fit but the other one doesn't, both books will get rejected because the agent or editor will think that overall you might not be a good match. If you do have a series in mind, include one sentence that says something to the effect that, "If you like my book, I think it would make a fabulous series."

- Don't compare your book to *Harry Potter* or the current #1 *New York Times* YA bestseller. Why not? Because everyone else will. You want your book to stand out as unique, and these references are so common they automatically lump your book in with the pack.

- Don't mention past rejections or other books you have written that you've not been able to sell. Start fresh and keep things positive.

- Don't submit to several people within the same publishing house or agency.

0123456789   +   ÷   —

- Don't resubmit the same work to an agent or editor who has rejected it unless it has been so substantially revised as to be considered a new work.

- Don't include your entire manuscript unless it's been requested.

MANUSCRIPT PREPARATION

So what happens if you get a bite? You've crafted the best possible query letter and an agent or editor writes you back and requests that you send your manuscript, or a partial sample. What next?

First of all, pat yourself on the back. Any time you hear from an agent or editor—even if it's just a handwritten note on a form rejection letter—it's good news. It means your query letter stood out and the idea for your novel sounds compelling enough that it warranted his personal attention.

Next, take a deep breath and remind yourself that a request from an agent or editor doesn't seal the deal. He still needs to read your work and decide it's the right match. Your job from this point on is to remove any obstacles that might stand between you and a contract.

The first obstacle is timely submission. Once an editor or agent requests your work, try to send it in a timely manner. Strike while the iron is hot. Believe it or not, we routinely requested material at Curtis Brown, Ltd., that arrived weeks or months after we asked to see it. By that time, the original query letter was forgotten, filed away, and the enthusiasm that prompted us to ask for the manuscript had dissipated. In its place was a lingering suspicion that the author had just finished her book and we'd be receiving a lightly edited first draft.

You'll want to send your manuscript as soon as possible after receiving the request, but you can certainly take a day or two to glance over it one more time to make sure it's ready to make the best possible first impression. I can generally read my whole book in a day if I need to, and if you have the time available, you might want to do one last check for misspellings, grammar mistakes, and sloppy wording. This is not a time for substantial editing—hopefully you've accomplished that before you started the submission process—but it is a time to look things over with an eye toward polishing your prose.

Check your manuscript format and make sure it meets the following criteria:

- double-spaced
- Times New Roman twelve-point font
- standard one-inch margins
- printed on white paper
- unbound
- your last name and the page number are listed on each page
- pages are clean and tidy
- no blank pages are inserted into the text

Always follow the guidelines for submission that an agency or publishing house provides, even if they conflict with what's written above. You want your work to meet their standards, and showing that you care enough to follow their stated policies will go a long way.

Once your book is ready to be sent out, write a short business letter to the agent or editor thanking him for requesting your material and reminding him of the relevant details of your novel and your writing credentials. Agents and editors deal with many books every day, so it never hurts to refresh their memory.

If you'd like to include a self-addressed stamped postcard with a line written on it that says, "We have received your manuscript," feel free to do so, although I'll warn you, at times your entire submission will end up on a pile until it's ready to be reviewed, so your postcard might not be returned to you until the package is opened. Also, be sure to include an SASE for the agent's or editor's response to your work. Make sure there's enough postage attached if you'd like your manuscript returned, otherwise it will most likely be recycled. Finally, when you put your package in the mail, write "Requested Material" on the outside so it can easily make it into the correct pile.

One question I was asked often when working at the literary agency was, "What do I do if the agent requests a certain number of pages and that page count leaves off mid-sentence or mid-scene? Is it okay to send more pages?" In this instance, yes. Including an extra page or two in order to complete a sentence or scene is generally fine. You might want to politely mention that you've done so in your letter. What's not acceptable is sending out far more material than the agent or editor asked for. He knows what he'd like to see, and it's up to him to decide if he wants to see more of your work based on the sample you've provided.

Another common question is, "When is it okay to follow up once I've sent my manuscript?" This question is a bit trickier. In my opinion, it's fine to follow up on your work as long as you do so politely and you wait an appropriate amount of time before your first and subsequent inquiries. If you haven't heard back from an agent or editor in one month's time and you want to call and verify *receipt* of your manuscript, ask for her assistant and keep your inquiry succinct. It's rare that an agent or editor will have read your book within one month, so you don't want to imply that you're being impatient.

If you then wait another two months after verifying receipt and still haven't gotten a response, it would be appropriate to call again, or to write a brief note asking if she's had a chance to review your work. Remember, you should always be professional during these interactions because how you present yourself will make an impression as to what kind of author you'd be to work with. Difficult as it might be to believe, I used to receive rude, disgruntled follow-up calls, and they almost inevitably prompted a rejection of the author's work. Following up too soon or too often shows a lack of understanding of the publishing field, and who wants to work with a client who is already demanding and difficult?

Should you receive a request for your manuscript from another agent or editor during the time you have it on submission, hold off on sending it until you've heard from the first one, or until you've notified the first one that you're withdrawing your submission. If you've been waiting on that first response for a while, a brief note or a call letting the agent or editor know that there is other interest, and inquiring as to when he might have a response for you, should prompt some action. Avoid submitting your work to multiple agents or editors without letting all parties know—you might find yourself in a sticky situation if more than one agent or editor expresses interest. Every connection is important in publishing, so don't burn any bridges.

NEGOTIATING A CONTRACT

The ideal end result of all this hard work is that an editor decides she loves your book and wants to offer you a contract. If so, congratulations! You've earned one of those few coveted spots on a publisher's list. But before you can proceed to working with your new editor, there's the small matter of a contract.

If you have an agent, it's his job to negotiate the advance, royalties, and terms of your book contract with your publishing house.

What generally happens is that an editor, when interested in buying your work, will approach your agent with an offer that includes the details of all the terms listed above. Your agent will then contact you and discuss the offer. He should take the time to explain what these terms mean and which parts of the offer can be improved. Don't hesitate to ask questions or offer your opinions! This is your book and your future.

Once you've had this discussion, your agent can then return to the publishing house and ask for modifications to the original offer. This process can go on for several rounds of negotiation before the final details of your contract get ironed out. Contracts might then take an additional four to six weeks to get drawn up and mailed to your agent for review.

But what happens if you don't have an agent? Negotiating your own contract is not something I would recommend, even if you have a spouse or a friend who is a lawyer. Unless he's specifically a publishing lawyer, there may be unique aspects to your contract he won't be familiar with. He may not know the industry standards for YA and might make unreasonable or too lenient demands. More than one editorial relationship has become strained before it even started by difficult contract negotiations between an editor and author, or an editor and an author's spouse.

Still, if you do decide this is the best option for you, I highly recommend reading as much about the subject as possible. There are entire books devoted to the subject of contract negotiation. The SCBWI once again provides related material for its members. Look on their Web site (www.scbwi.org) for their eight-page document entitled *Answers to Some Questions About Contracts* and their *Sample Children's Book Contracts*.

The Authors Guild is also a great resource (www.authorsguild. org). They offer their members a free sixty-four-page reference guide to negotiating contracts called *Authors Guild Model Trade Book Contract and Guide,* along with seminars on contract negotiation and free contract reviews.

I won't attempt to cover all of the relevant information in one small section of this book, but I will provide you with a primer so you're familiar with the terms used in contracts and you'll know what points you want to pay special attention to. Even if you have an agent, it would be worth your time to familiarize yourself with these definitions so you'll be able to understand what's happening throughout the negotiation process.

Here are some basic contract terms every author ought to know:

Grant of Rights. This clause specifies who controls the rights to your book. The copyright to your work should almost always belong to you, unless you're negotiating a work-for-hire agreement where you sell all rights and have no further say over how the publisher uses the material. Otherwise, you control the copyright and you grant the publisher specific rights, such as the right to print, publish, and sell your book. Rights can be exclusive—meaning only one party can control them at a time—or nonexclusive, meaning you can sell them to multiple parties. Most publishers want exclusive rights. Rights can also be relegated to certain territories. For example, a publisher might ask for exclusive world rights, but you might only agree to sell them exclusive rights to publish the material in the United States, Canada, and their territories. Rights can also be limited by language. You can sell English language rights or specific foreign language rights. Which rights you grant to your publisher should depend on who has the best opportunity to exploit those rights to your benefit.

Subrights. Subrights refer to all the forms your novel might take other than a traditional hardcover or paperback book. Think of all the formats stories take in our society. There are movies, plays, TV adaptations, audiobooks, book club editions, foreign editions, magazine excerpts, electronic downloads, reprints, merchandizing. These rights can be licensed to outside parties, either by you or your publisher, depending on who controls the subrights as stated in your contract.

Advance. Your advance is the amount of money your publisher will pay you up front, either upon signing of the contract or in some other split that your contract specifies. (Often contracts state that the advance will be paid with one portion on signing of the contract and another portion on delivery and acceptance of the final edited manuscript; sometimes a third portion will be paid on publication.) It's important to note that the full term is "advance against royalties," meaning that whatever you've been paid up front will be deducted from the profit you make on royalties later on. You'll need to earn back your advance before you receive any royalty money.

Royalties. Royalties are a percentage of the retail price (or net price, depending on what your contract specifies) you'll receive for each copy of your book that is sold. Generally, royalties escalate slightly, so as you sell more copies of your books you also receive a higher percentage of the sales. Not only will different royalty rates apply to hardcover and paperback sales, but there will also be specific royalty rates for books sold through nontraditional means, such as books that are exported, sold at a "deep discount," or ordered through the mail.

Accounting and Audit Clauses. Your contract should specify when you will receive your royalty statements (for many publishers it's twice a year) and should provide you with the right to have an outside party audit the publisher's books if you suspect a discrepancy in their bookkeeping.

Option Clause. This is a very important clause in any contract and most people try to strike it out entirely if possible. The option clause says you are obligated to submit your next work to your publisher. This does not mean your publisher has to buy it. What makes this clause so dangerous to authors is it can tie up your work so you can't freely submit it to another publishing house, and if you are unhappy with your original publishing house it makes it that much more difficult to leave. If you cannot get the option clause removed from your contract, be sure to use language that only refers to one book, and at the very least try to limit this to the exact type of book you're obligated to submit for your publisher's first refusal. For example, you would want to be sure the option only applied to your next book for teens, and not a picture book or adult book you might decide to write later on.

Author Copies. Believe it or not, authors do not get unlimited free copies of their own books. It's sad, but true. Your contract will specify exactly how many copies of each format of your book you're entitled to, and after that you'll have to purchase copies, usually at a discount. Most contracts offer ten free copies, but you will probably want to negotiate for more since you can imagine how quickly those copies disappear, especially if you're using them for promotion.

0123456789 + ÷ ▬

Approval and Consultation. These terms exist in some contracts and grant the author the right to be consulted on issues surrounding cover art, subsidiary rights sales, or grants of permissions.

Warranties and Indemnities. This clause has to do with legal responsibility in the event that you are accused of plagiarizing another writer's work, or should a legal suit be brought against you and your publisher for any reason (for example, libel). Usually the clause states who will pay for the legal costs of such a proceeding (generally a percentage split between you and the publisher, provided you're not found guilty).

Publication Date. This is more important than it might sound. Although your contract won't include an exact publication date, it should include language that says that the publisher must publish your book within a certain amount of time (often eighteen months after delivery and acceptance of your manuscript). Without publication language, your publisher could tie up the rights to your work indefinitely, always promising to publish your book but never delivering on their promise. And if you have an option clause that says something about submitting your next book "after publication," you could be in trouble!

Is your head spinning yet? Contracts can be overwhelming, and it's important to be as detailed as possible so the language used within them can cover any circumstances that might arise. The definitions above only scratch the surface of this topic, but the good news is there are plenty of resources available to help you out. In addition to The Authors Guild and SCBWI, check your local bookstore for titles that will further your knowledge. Be sure to read reviews on Amazon.com or ask for recommendations so you get the best possible information on the subject.

Homework:

Draft three versions of a query letter, varying your tone and content in each. Choose five people to read all of the letters and ask them to choose the one they like best. Have them underline their favorite lines from each letter and circle their least favorite lines. Which version did most people prefer? Can you use the best lines from each letter and eliminate the weakest lines from your final version?

9th PERIOD
SHOP CLASS
Getting Your Hands Dirty: Teen Sex, Drugs, Slang, Technology, and Marketing Your Book

How many of you took some version of shop class when you were in school? In ninth grade, I took a computer class, meant to give us hands-on experience with programming DOS (how dated is that?!). I'm sure my teacher would be dismayed to learn that my most vivid memory from this class is printing out long sheets of scrolled paper with lists of the nicknames my best friend and I used for all the boys in our grade. My memories of wood shop have fared a little bit better. Here, I recall using the skill saw to cut puzzle shapes and building model bridges that could hold our body weight. But really, what I most remember from both of these classes—and from every other class I took that fell under the elective category of "shop"—was the opportunity they provided to interact with an entirely different set of kids than my normal schedule allowed.

Shop classes have always been great levelers. Kids on the honors track and kids pursuing technical careers worked side by side, learning the secrets that skilled trades have to offer. There was always an air of the real world to shop classes. The teachers seemed different—less concerned with philosophy and more focused on the practical, everyday concerns of their subject matter. Shop class wasn't about theory, it was about facts. Here, you learned the way the world *really* worked and made decisions to apply this knowledge accordingly.

When it comes to writing books for teens, it's important that authors understand both the philosophical aspects of creating quality literature for teenagers and the practical realities of writing and marketing your books for this age group—realities like varied expectations from kids and adults, and the difficult choices authors have to make about content in teen fiction.

When you're writing for teenagers there are plenty of "rules" that others are ready to impose on your books. These range from literary rules, like keeping abreast of slang and technology in order to keep your books sounding current, to moral rules, like avoiding swear words or sex scenes in order not to corrupt impressionable young people. Break one of these rules and your book is apt to be shunned or banned, at least by a certain percentage of your audience.

On the other hand, there are those who might avoid your books precisely because you keep the rules! Can you realistically portray teens today without swearing or alluding to sex? Will teenagers want to read books that don't accurately reflect the world they live in? Won't your story suffer if you modify it in a false way to please other people?

And at the end of this whole process will it be the parent or the teen who picks your book up off the shelf? Should you appeal to the high school librarian or the high school student? How can you reach actual teenage readers with your work?

Shop class is our chance to turn theory into practice before our time together comes to an end. It's time to talk directly about sex, drugs, swearing, and every other hot-button issue you'll confront as you write and market your book to young adults. And then it's time to get that book into the hands of teen readers, which is what you've intended all along.

WHO IS YOUR AUDIENCE, *REALLY*?

By now we've come full circle—back to the question of audience. Remember when we defined teen literature as books written for and marketed to teens? How, then, can there be any question now as to who you're writing for? On one level, there isn't. Your audience is exactly who we've said it was all along: teenagers. But on another level, when you write for teens you need to deal with the dual nature of who buys, stocks, promotes, reviews, and possibly bans your books. Most often, these people are adults.

Many times adults act as gatekeepers to what teens read, watch, and listen to. This is true for several reasons. For one thing, teens are usually still at an age where they're living with their parents or other family members who take care of them. They have not yet achieved independence either financially or emotionally. Since parents or guardians are responsible for guiding teens into the adult world, they often limit what they can experience either in real life or vicariously through TV, movies, and literature.

At the same time, if you think back to first-period history class, you'll remember that teens have often been on the cutting edge of change—challenging the boundaries adults set for them, pushing the limits of their freedom and independence. Many teens are looking for books that reflect the world as *they* see it, and that world is increasingly complex.

So how does an author navigate these waters?

This is where our definition of literature becomes very important. Literature is usually defined as writings that are valued for their form in addition to their content. When referring to literature we tend to think of classic novels, poetry, or plays as opposed to journalism or technical writings.

Many authors also come up with their own definitions of literature. We each have our intent as novelists, and that intent might be to make people laugh, to entertain, or to illuminate. I would argue that if your intent is to inform, you come dangerously close to producing work that falls outside the boundaries of literature. Not that there's anything wrong with journalism or technical writing—both can be written exceedingly well—but as a novelist, you need to think about form, not didacticism.

What this means to me is that decisions about the inclusion of controversial issues such as sex, bad language, character drug use, or negative behaviors need to be made in the context of the story itself, looking first and foremost at what is necessary to write the best possible book rather than looking to promote either a moral agenda or controversy for the sake of controversy.

What makes something the best possible book?

Everyone gets to answer this on their own, but for me, the very best books shed light on human nature and show us some corner of ourselves that we either never knew existed or have long ignored. These books illuminate our world so we see it as it truly is, even if that truth is shown by contrasting reality with fantasy. The best books draw us in and make us feel something—we laugh or cry, and maybe we do both at the exact same time. The best books teach us something about our lives, but this kind of learning doesn't come as a lesson or an informational tract. It arrives through vicarious experience as we accompany the characters in a book through the world the author has created.

The question then, for each of us, is: What kind of world are we looking to create? Are we hoping to move our readers through realism, fantasy, or some combination of the two? As you think about the teenage world you're portraying, consider what realities would be a part of your character's world. Do drugs exist? If so, how close or how distant would they be to your character's experience? Would sexual feelings or sexual experiences be a part of your character's life? How would the characters speak in the environment you've chosen?

Many authors get confused and try to portray a potential reader's experience, or their own views or wishes, rather than remembering that the world that exists on the pages of a book belongs to the characters. Limitations should not be imposed based on the author's desires, or even a potential reader's desires. When that happens, worlds collide and the spell of great fiction is broken.

To give you an example of what I'm referring to, I'll use my own experiences with controversy. In *Fat Kid Rules the World*, the main character, Troy Billings, is a junior in high school who is living in Manhattan and finds entrée into the alternative world of punk rock. In this world, I felt that Troy would naturally hear and use language that some people consider offensive. Since he's a teenage boy, I also felt that sexual feelings would be a part of his reality, even if sex itself wasn't. Furthermore, I felt that he'd not only be aware of drugs, but he would most likely be confronted with them up close and personal at one time or another.

Despite what some people might suggest, I didn't make the decision to include bad language, sexual feelings, or drugs in my book in an arbitrary manner, to add "spice" or controversy to my novel. Personally,

I rarely swear and I don't use or advocate the use of drugs, but when I wrote this book it wasn't *my* world I was portraying; it was Troy's. I wasn't willing to portray Troy's world as I, or anyone else, *wished* it might be. Instead I chose to portray it as I believe it truly would be. Should someone argue with the realism of that portrayal, I would have to be called to task, but if, in fact, I've done my job, hopefully I've opened a window to a world that most of us don't usually get to peer into—that of a six-foot-one, three hundred-pound, punk rock drummer in New York City.

My goal when I was writing was to create this world in a realistic way, and my hope was that people would go on a journey with the characters and, regardless of how they might personally feel about the lives portrayed, they would come to love them. After all, isn't this what life is all about? Seeing other people, places, and beliefs and accepting them for what they are rather than trying to change them into . . . *us*?

In my next book, *The Liberation of Gabriel King*, which was geared to younger readers instead of teens, my characters are fourth-grade students living in Georgia in 1976. In this book you'll find no references to sex or drugs and no swear words. In this world, the insertion of swear words, drugs, or sexual feelings would have been out of place—imposed on the text. But what you will find is the word "nigger" used by an adult and overheard by the children.

This book deals with racism, and the characters must struggle with the confusing and unfair nature of the world they live in. Since the story takes place at a time in our country's history when the civil rights movement was still new, it seemed to me that racism would certainly be a part of these children's everyday lives. Yes, the temptation to rewrite history was there. I don't find it any easier than the next person to accept the uglier realities of the world we live in, but what would be gained by whitewashing the past and what opportunities might be lost to discuss the present?

What it comes right down to is portraying the world you've chosen with the most skill, artistry, and truth possible. Had I chosen a fantasy setting for either of these novels—an otherworldly punk rock zone in some far distant galaxy, or two kids living in the southern part of a country that never existed—I could have created these worlds with no limitations imposed by the real world. I could have created universes where different races had always existed in harmony, or a planet where sex was something teenagers never experienced, wondered about, or grappled with. But those aren't the settings I chose.

Likewise, in the modern world I might have decided to portray a different type of teenager in *Fat Kid Rules the World*. Perhaps, I might have chosen a very sheltered six-foot-one, three hundred-pound teen boy who never swore and refused to get involved in the punk rock scene because he objected to the drug use and swearing, but what a different book that would be!

Each author must make her choices about the book she wants to write. What is your premise? Who are your characters? Where is your book set? When is your book set? These choices will inform your decisions about what language and issues exist in your story. No agenda, either pro or con, can do anything but draw from the integrity of your novel.

SLANG, TECHNOLOGY, AND FADS

If sex, drugs, and bad language present types of difficulties when writing for teens, dealing with slang, technology, and fads present a whole different can of worms. Here, it's not the protective, judging eyes of adults you need to be concerned with, but the sharp, assessing eyes of teens themselves. The modern world changes very rapidly, and just about the time you've filled your book with all the "hip" references you can muster, you'll probably find some teen snickering at you, saying, "Did she just say 'hip'? No one says 'hip' anymore!"

The same is true of technology. The moment you think you've been clever by incorporating the newest technological gadget, another greatly improved one is sure to come along. Computers, cell phones, iPods … all of these are evolving right before our eyes, and new inventions we could never have imagined are just moments away from being thrust into the marketplace.

Staying abreast of what's happening in the world is important. You certainly don't want to make outdated references in a modern novel, but it's also important not to let the quest for relevance outweigh your characters and plot. Remember, it's the timeless aspects of a book that will make a reader want to keep reading, not the references to what's new and fashionable.

When you *do* need to refer to a cultural phenomenon—whether it's a celebrity, a musical group, a technological invention, a fashion piece, or a slang word—you can handle it in several different ways.

First, you can choose to accept your limitations. Some books are going to become dated. There will always be classics that seem as relevant today as they did when they were written—so much so that you might unconsciously remember them as if they took place today even though the setting might have been decades prior—but there are other books that are meant to capture a specific moment in time and their intent is to appeal to fast-paced modern readers who are interested in what's hot *right now*.

One example of these sorts of books would be the novels that came out right about the time when the Internet was becoming popular and used the e-mail format as something new and seductive to teen readers. Looking at many of these novels now, in the age of instant messaging and MySpace pages, they often seem simple and dated in terms of their technological references, but for the authors who wrote these books, the current appeal outweighed the future chance of the technology becoming obsolete or being replaced by something newer or better.

Another way to handle the ever-changing cultural scene is to invent a new one, unique to your book. Depending on what type of book you're writing, this may or may not work for you, but some authors have pulled it off brilliantly. In the futuristic novel *Rash* by Pete Hautman, the author invents new slang, popular foods, technology, clothes … everything you can think of that makes a teenager cool. The same is true for M.T. Anderson's *Feed*, which also takes place in the future.

But what about contemporary novels? There's no reason you can't invent popular fads in a book that takes place today. Want to reference a well-known music group? Make it a local group that all the kids love. Having difficulty choosing a wardrobe for your fashion-conscious character? Give her the type of fashion sense that's both personal and eclectic, or make up some fabulous new item she finds on a trip to Soho.

Finally, you can take the approach of choosing the classics. When it comes to fashion, celebrities, movies, and music there will always be certain references that will stand the test of time. How do you know? Because they already have. The Beatles might not be the "new" thing anymore, but if your character loves them you can guarantee kids will know who they are and the reference will have meaning. One word of warning, though. Too many classic references can get old real quick.

Another one of my pet peeves in teen novels is that so many characters watch and adore classic, black-and-white films, while in real life I know of very few teens who actually watch them. It's the equivalent of giving your character red hair and green eyes. Are there people out there with red hair and green eyes? Certainly, but the literary usage has become so common as to be cliché.

I'd suggest you use some mix of all these techniques to give your novel a timeless feel. And of course, your choices will have to be defined by the characters and the setting. For some books, the issue of modern relevance—or the hip factor—simply won't matter, either because the book is historical or because the character is withdrawn from the modern world, paying no attention to what's popular and what is not.

WHAT, IF ANYTHING, DO YOU FIND OFFENSIVE IN TEEN NOVELS? SHOULD BOOKS BE BANNED IF THEY CONTAIN OBJECTIONABLE CONTENT?

Teen Panel

Stephanie, age 17, Florida: No!!! Do not ban them. People are only afraid of what they don't understand and thus they label it "controversial." And that is when it becomes what they label it to be. Teenagers naturally want to rebel; it's in the genetics and makeup of being a teen. So when someone speaks the words "it's bad for you" or "you shouldn't be reading that" . . . in teen language that's carte blanche to read it, which just adds to publicity and the nonsense. What I do find offensive in teen novels is the excessive descriptions of sexual encounters . . . it makes me think "Come on people, do it don't write it . . . Don't you have better things to do than imagine it?" I guess, I think it just takes away from the novel, and instead of building it, crushes it.

Dana, age 12, Maine: If that means swearing, drugs, sex or anything like that, then yes, they should be banned.

Oscar, age 15, New Mexico: In my opinion, I think there is nothing that you can't put in teen novels because everything has already been embraced in real life by teens, like drugs, gangs, sex, violence, etc.

Regan, age 13, Maine: I hate it when in books teens have horrible relationships with their parents. I don't like this because I don't feel it represents most teenagers. I feel that a majority of kids have very strong relationships with their parents. I understand when there are small conflicts and small disagreements, but I don't think it is an out and out battle all the time. I don't think books should be banned for this material, I just wish that authors would understand what I'm saying.

Machele, age 15, New York: Books should not be banned. Parents should talk to their children about the situation instead.

Kathleen, age 17, New York: I don't think books should be banned for "objectionable content." After all, objectionable is relative and everyone has a different definition. If anything, make a small note of content that may be found objectionable somewhere, like on the inside of the book flap. That way, people could choose their reading material without anything being banned.

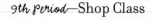

> Jose, age 15, New Mexico: I don't find anything in a teen novel offensive because I believe being a teenager means discovering the realities of the world, so anything like profanity or any adult content is part of being a teenager and becoming an adult.

BUT WHAT ABOUT *YOU*?

Of course, it might be well and good for your character to be withdrawn from the modern world, but what about you? As an author for teen readers, do you need to stay current, accessing teens through all the latest technologies and presenting yourself as the literary equivalent of Justin Timberlake? (Let's see how quickly that reference becomes dated!)

This is a difficult question. If you're J.K. Rowling, do you need to focus on your image and invest yourself in promotion? Nope. At this point, I doubt she needs to do any marketing of her books or of herself as an author. Her books are selling quite well on their own, thank you. But for the rest of us, promoting ourselves to teen readers can be a challenge as we discover the world of forums, blogs, Web sites, book trailers, and podcasts.

Although it is your publisher's job to sell your book once it's produced, you can't sit back and wait for a bestseller. Or even a decent seller. For most of us, it's necessary to join in the process of marketing our teen novels through personal appearances and online resources. The good news is, new technologies are making it possible for us to reach teens in a more direct manner than ever before. They offer us opportunities for publicity that are not dependent on our publisher's limited budgets.

PERSONAL APPEARANCES

Personal appearances can run the gamut from author visits to schools and libraries, speeches, workshops, and bookstore signings to visiting a college class as a guest lecturer or doing a reading at a book festival. Depending on your level of comfort speaking in public, you'll need to gauge how many of these visits you want to do per year and how actively you pursue these opportunities.

If you're interested in making personal appearances a part of your publicity repertoire, a good place to start when you first get published is the local level. Contact your community bookstore, especially if you have an independent bookstore nearby, and see if you can set up a book signing. Chances are the store will be open to this idea, but you will probably need to send out some of your own invitations to the event. When I worked at the Merritt Bookstore in Cold Spring, New York, I found that the most successful events were the ones where the authors played an active role, sending out invitations to friends and family. It's difficult for a small store to generate large crowds, so if you want people to attend your event, help out by publicizing your visit.

Local schools and libraries may also be open to hosting a visiting author. You can contact them with a formal business letter, or if you have a friend who might put in a good word for you, that's even better. You might also consider printing a small flier with your biographical information, some information about your presentation, and the name and ISBN of your book(s). Fliers can be expensive if done professionally, but the return is often worth the money spent. You can also print something on your own using the publishing software offered on most computers. Consider purchasing a mailing list as well. Most printing places offer mailing lists tailored to your specifications.

Want to do school or library visits within a one hundred-mile radius of where you live? You might be surprised to find out how many schools and libraries you've never even heard of.

I'd also recommend you offer to do your first few school or library visits for free so you can work out your presentation and establish references. Once you have a firm footing, you can set a fair price based both on what you feel you have to offer and on what most schools and libraries in your area can afford. Fees for author visits vary dramatically ranging from token amounts like fifty or one hundred dollars that just cover your costs and might leave you with a little bit extra, to fifteen hundred to two thousand dollars that award-winning authors with a long track record might receive. Remember that your fee should change according to how many presentations you're doing (you might do one presentation for a library or up to three separate presentations for a school visit), the length of time you're asked to present for, and the size of the program. I highly recommend you iron out all of these details in writing at the time you schedule the event.

Unlike school visits, library visits, and bookstore signings, it's a little more difficult to pursue keynote speeches, workshops, and panels at conferences. Most of the time, the coordinators of the larger conferences such as those hosted by the SCBWI, the American Library Association (ALA), the National Council of Teachers of English (NCTE), Writer's Digest Books, or BookExpo America, will want to contact you or your publisher, not the other way around. However, if you can find out the name of a conference coordinator there's probably no harm in submitting your resume and pitching your idea for a speech or workshop. SCBWI hosts regional conferences in addition to their large annual conferences, and they just might be looking for a workshop exactly like the one you have in mind.

If you're very eager to book speaking engagements, make sure your name is listed in as many speakers directories as possible. If you follow the path of traditional publishing, your publisher will probably have an author coordinator on staff, and she will most likely list information about the programs their authors offer. Make sure to introduce yourself to this person and double check that your name is listed on any Web site they maintain. SCBWI offers a directory listing public speakers, and in my area, the New England Booksellers Association publishes a directory every two years. Chances are there's something similar in your area, too. Forums (which we'll discuss more in a moment) also provide opportunities to share personalized tips and exchange information with other writers. Every area of the country offers unique opportunities that other YA writers may already have access to.

WEB SITES

What if you're not comfortable with public speaking? Are there other ways to publicize your books that don't require you to stand in front of an audience? Certainly. We're fortunate in this day and age to have plenty of opportunities available through the Internet. Web sites can be created at an affordable cost, and I highly recommend maintaining one. They're great ways for teens to find out more about you and your books.

Obviously, the easiest way to procure a Web site is to ask a friend, family member, or acquaintance who knows how to create them. Many people can build Web sites these days—if you have a teenager in your family, you might start by asking him. The Authors Guild also offers free Web sites to new members, although this offer won't continue indefinitely. Still, it's a great deal while it lasts, and even if you're not a new member or the offer expires, their normal Web site design and hosting costs are very reasonable.

If you don't know someone who can design a site, you can also go to your local chamber of commerce and look for Web designers. As with anything, you want to be careful to choose someone reputable to work with. It's easy to get taken advantage of, so don't be afraid to ask for references. You should plan to meet with several designers, and before you speak with them try to determine how you envision your site and what you'd like the site to do for you. Come up with different statements about what you want and need. Examples might be:

- "I want a site that can promote my books."
- "I want a Web site where teens can have fun."
- "I want a Web site where teachers and librarians can find resources."

Ask plenty of questions and make sure the person you're speaking to is able to explain her work in terms you understand. Find out how she handles updates to sites because author Web sites tend to change as each new book or review is available.

Make sure your Web designer will provide hosting and register your domain name. Hosting for Web sites is the equivalent of renting office space for your business. A Web site needs bandwidth to exist, and those who "host" sites do so for a fee. Your domain name is the name that points people to your site, such as *klgoing.com* or *fatkidrulestheworld.com*. It is very important that your domain name be registered in YOUR name and not in the name of the person who creates your Web site. Your domain belongs to you, and should you decide to change Web designers, you'll need to be in control. You'll also want to be clear on whose responsibility it is to renew your domain name *before* it expires so you don't lose it.

Depending on how large a site you want, you can expect to pay anywhere from several hundred to several thousand dollars to develop a Web site. While it might seem like choosing a free site or a low-cost site is the obvious way to go, don't discount sites that cost more to develop. Many Web sites contain beautiful graphics, but they don't attract browsers because they don't have the text that search engines are looking for. You want to build a successful Web site that will meet your expectations, rather than simply posting a page online that might or might not attract readers.

FORUMS

Forums are online venues for conversation. When you go to a forum, you'll find multiple topics posted that are awaiting readers' responses. You can click on any topic and read what people have to say. Forums can be large and complex with many different topics in many different categories, or they can be relatively small and simple. You can reply to a particular topic (called a thread) or to an individual response (called a post). You can even post your own topic and see how others respond to you.

I maintain a small forum on my Web site (www.klgoing.com/forums). It offers me a chance to interact with my readers by posting about common interests. My categories are broad because the forum is designed for any reader who'd like to participate. For my purposes, I've found that sticking with general categories like books, movies, current events, and writing works just fine. Within each category people have posted many different threads. For example, in the "Books" category someone might start a thread about whatever book he just finished reading. He could ask if others have read it and what they thought, and then other people can post their responses. Topics that have recent posts move to the top of the list, so someone can post on an old topic if it's one they'd like to bring back to people's attention or they can post something new and their thread will appear at the top of the list. You're welcome to visit me on my forum and practice posting! I'd love to hear about the projects you're working on and the books you love.

My forum is a good one to start out on if you're feeling nervous because many forums are much larger than mine. If you're comfortable with posting, there are quite a few forums specifically designed for adults trying to become published writers. Check out the SCBWI forum if you're a member, or the Absolute Write Water Cooler (www. absolutewrite.com/forums). Author Verla Kay hosts a forum called the Children's Writer's and Illustrator's Chat Board that's very popular with children's book writers (www.verlakay.com/boards). Sites such as these offer valuable opportunities to network with other writers, and they have many different categories for discussion including topics like "the craft of writing," "publicity and promotion," "legal questions," and "submission to agents and editors." There are even places to share your rejection letters.

You'd be surprised at how generous most writers are with information and how much you'll learn from participating in a forum. You might even find a critique group or link up with someone who's willing to serve as a reader for your manuscript. Forums might seem overwhelming at first, but remember, you don't have to post anything immediately. You can start by reading through the various threads, old and new, and when you feel ready you can reply to others or ask your own questions.

SOCIAL NETWORKING

Connecting with others is so important. Ask almost anyone and they will tell you that the key to success in most fields is networking. But what if you don't have a ton of connections? How can you realistically expect to meet and greet people from all across the country? This is where social networking sites come into play. Popular sites like MySpace, Facebook, and Friendster allow you to create a personal profile complete with photographs and information about yourself, and you can join groups with other people who share common interests. You can also add friends to your page and visit other people's pages, leaving them public comments or personal messages. These sites are great ways to connect directly to your fans no matter where they are, and they're a perfect way to get to know a large number of people all across the country.

But do they really offer anything other than distraction? Personally, I've gotten newspaper articles, an interview in an online magazine, multiple interviews with online book clubs, and invitations to visit libraries from my MySpace page. I've also made countless friends. I even applied for a job based on an opportunity I saw publicized in one of the groups I belong to. A friend of mine received a request for his manuscript from a well-known editor because he'd posted a comment on a mutual friend's page. The opportunities are literally endless since new people are joining every day.

The best part, though, is the chance to meet your fans in a more personal way. I love looking at the pages teens have designed for themselves. The variety is incredible. Teenagers include so much information (too much sometimes!) and you have a chance to see how they describe themselves, what they list as their favorite books, movies, and music, and many times they write blogs that are set as "public," meaning they are open to any reader. Interacting with the kids who contact me through my MySpace page has got to be one of the greatest thrills of being a YA author.

BLOGS

So what are blogs anyway? This is a good question and one that every writer should know the answer to. Blogging has become extremely popular, and it's fabulous publicity both to be mentioned in someone else's blog or to maintain your own.

For those of you who don't know, the term *blog* is short for web log. Basically, blogs are online journals that offer readers a chance to interact by posting comments about what the blogger has written. You can blog about anything from personal thoughts to book reviews to politics, and you can blog as frequently or as infrequently as you'd like. Personally, I don't have a lot of extra time, so my entries tend to be sporadic, but since the subjects I write about don't have any time limits, people can access any blog from my archive as well as my most current entry.

For writers who are devoted bloggers, blogs can offer an outlet for feelings, a chance to share your views with the world, an opportunity to interact with others, and one more way for you to share something personal with your fans. Many blogs are specialized as well. There are blogs devoted specifically to the discussion of books, or to library issues, or to any other subject under the sun.

There are many different online places available to host your blog if you'd like to keep one. Social networking sites such as MySpace usually offer a blog as part of your personal page. In addition, sites like LiveJournal, Open Diary, Blogger, WordPress, and GoogleLive all host blogs, in addition to myriad other sites too numerous to name.

PODCASTS, VIDEO CLIPS, AND BOOK TRAILERS

While most bloggers are still using the typed format, there are some who are using their video cameras to keep video blogs, otherwise know as vlogs. Video bloggers, or vloggers, might post their entries on YouTube or on their personal Web sites or social networking pages. Vlogging, like blogging, is yet another creative way you can reach out to your fans if you have the technology available.

Likewise, podcasts are simple and easy if you have modern computer equipment, including a microphone for your computer. Podcasts are audio clips that listeners can link to through various Web sites. They can be about any topic you choose. Some authors record podcasts about their writing process. Others might tell a personal story they want to share with their readers. When my third book, *Saint Iggy*, was due out, Harcourt asked me to do a podcast to share a little bit about where the story idea had come from and to read a chapter for my listeners. Some publishers have offered a series of podcasts interviewing various authors or asking multiple authors to respond to a similar question. Readers who visited their Web sites were then able to listen to the podcasts of their choice. They got a sense of the author's voice and personality, as well as additional insights into their books.

Finally, if you're really technically savvy, you can make your own book trailer. Book trailers are just like movie trailers, only they advertise your book. My husband and I made a book trailer for my fourth novel, *The Garden of Eve*, using our handheld camera and his computer editing program. There are also various services available where people will make a trailer for you, and these range in cost from minimal amounts like one hundred dollars to very expensive amounts. I read an article about one author who spent ten thousand dollars on his book trailer. Personally, I wouldn't recommend this. Book trailers are new and it's not yet proven whether they can positively affect sales. They are a lot of fun, however. So if you can make one yourself or can find someone who will do a good job for a small fee, they can be a great addition to your Web site and an avenue for potential readers to find you on YouTube.

GIVEAWAYS

Everyone loves free stuff. Teens are no exception. In some instances your publisher will distribute some sort of free promotional item in connection with your book, such as a bookmark or postcard, but other times, you might want to create something yourself. I've had bumper stickers made so I could hand them out at book signings and author visits. They promote my books, look cool, and are an eye-catching addition to my display. Other authors I know have distributed pens, pencils, stickers, temporary tattoos, bookmarks, and mouse pads. Do an online search or ask for recommendations from other authors to find out the best places for purchasing giveaway materials of your choice.

ARTICLES AND ESSAYS

You might find that after you're published you get asked to write short articles or essays for various publications. For example, I was asked to write a 500-word response to a question about English curriculum for a journal that circulates to English teachers. These are great opportunities to get your name out there to a large crowd who may not be familiar with your work.

If no one approaches you, try contacting magazines or newspapers you think might include something you've written. Perhaps you can write an article for your local newspaper about authors living in your area, or books you recommend for teens. Since larger teen magazines like *Seventeen* and *Teen Vogue* are hard to break into, try looking for smaller magazines or online magazines and sending them a query letter pitching your idea.

Writing articles and essays builds name recognition, and once someone knows and likes your writing style they will probably pick up one of your books. This can be time consuming, but the payoff might be worth the distraction from your novel writing. Consider the venue, its readership, and its circulation before making your decisions about which projects to pursue.

REACHING TEEN READERS

Throughout this discussion of tough issues and promotion, it's necessary to continually come back to why we're doing all this. Reaching teen readers is what being an author of books for teenagers is all about. It's what motivated you to become a YA author right from the start, and it's what will make the process of researching, writing, publishing, and marketing your books worthwhile in the end. Sales are important, yes, but it's the teens who read and respond to your work who both create the marketplace and fulfill it.

Writing for teenagers is never an easy task. It's as complex as creating work in any field, with the added twist of navigating different audiences—adult parents, booksellers, librarians, and reviewers, along with the teens themselves—but in the end this is also what can make this field the most rewarding.

Remember that quote from Bruce Brooks? "Young adults deserve our best regard and our best literature."

It takes a great deal of hard work to bring a manuscript from the idea phase, to the development phase, to the editing phase, and finally to the point of being a complete bound book, but if you can say at the end of this process that you've been a part of providing the best literature to young adults today, then there is no question your efforts have been worthwhile.

Homework: You might be expecting your final homework assignment to have something to do with building a Web site, posting on a forum, or maybe even recording a podcast, but this isn't the case.

Your final homework assignment is to celebrate the hard work you've put in during the course of this book.

Writing can be a long and solitary process, and too often the moments of recognition are few and far between. If I can leave you with one thought let it be this: Celebrate each and every milestone you achieve. Reward yourself for having the drive to read this book from start to finish. Go for a walk or out to dinner, buy that new novel you've been itching to read, or go to the movies. Whatever you choose, remember that writing is a journey that ought to be joyous, and you are moving forward along the path. Take the time to congratulate yourself on every goal you reach.

 Writing & Selling the *ya novel*

index

Writing & Selling the *ya novel*

Writing & Selling the *ya novel*